# LEARN TO BE AN AGENT OF CHANGE

SALES SECRETS FOR TODAY'S EXECUTIVES

# SELLING CHANGE

*101+ Secrets for Growing Sales*

*by*

*Leading Change*

**BRETT CLAY**

Published by Ariva Publishing
244 Madison Avenue, Suite 7100
New York, NY 10016
www.arivapublishing.com



Distributed by Greenleaf Book Group LLC

For ordering information, please contact Greenleaf Book Group LLC at PO Box 91869, Austin, TX 78709, 512.891.6100.

For volume discounts on corporate purchases, please contact Ariva Publishing at 244 Madison Ave, Suite 7100, New York, NY 10016, 646.706.7129.

Illustrations by Rick Evans
Cover design by Greenleaf Book Group
Interior design and composition by Kimberly Martin
Every attempt has been made to source all quotes properly.

Publisher's Cataloging-in-Publication

Clay, Brett.
Selling change: 101+ secrets for growing sales by leading change / Brett Clay. -- 1st ed.
p. cm.
At head of title: Sales secrets for today's executives.
LCCN 2009901725
ISBN-13: 978-0-9822952-3-6
ISBN-10: 0-9822952-3-5

1. Selling. 2. Selling--Psychological aspects. 3. Change (Psychology) I. Title. II. Title: At head of title: Sales secrets for today's executives.

HF5438.25.C53 2009 658.85
QBI09-600007



Part of the Tree Neutral™ program, which offsets the number of trees consumed in the production and printing of this book by taking proactive steps, such as planting trees in direct proportion to the number of trees used: www.treeneutral.com

Printed in the United States of America on acid-free paper

09 10 11 12 13 14 10 9 8 7 6 5 4 3 2 1

First Edition

## DEDICATION

To my wonderful wife and children who are
my sources of unending support and joy.

To you, the reader, whose challenges and courage
I truly admire: It is my honor and privilege to help you
achieve the changes you desire!

# CONTENTS

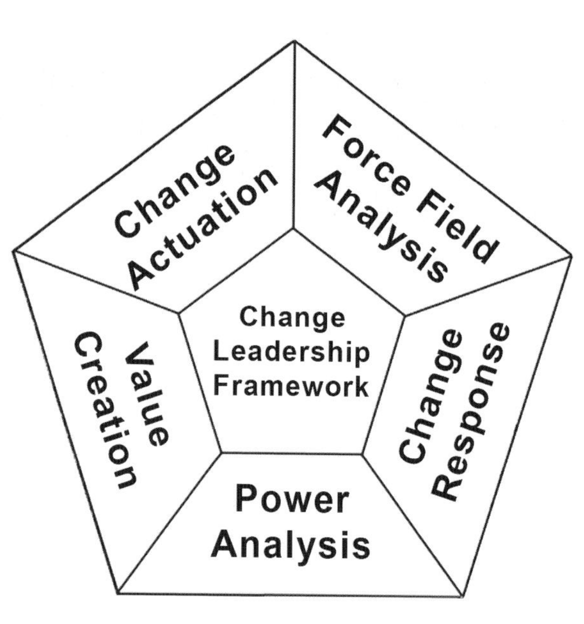
Change Actuation
Force Field Analysis
Change Leadership Framework
Value Creation
Change Response
Power Analysis

# INTRODUCTION

## THE CHANGE IMPERATIVE

# INTRODUCTION

## TO

# THE CHANGE IMPERATIVE

### Why You Need This Book

It is often said that change is constant. But, in today's world, change is imperative. To succeed in business in the 21st century, salespeople and their companies must not only adapt to change, they must lead change, driving real outcomes on behalf of their customers.

> "Change is not merely necessary to life — it is life." — Alvin Toffler

This book will show you how to survive and thrive among the tremendous changes affecting the sales profession and the companies that employ salespeople. You will learn:

- The five disciplines that will make you and your company invaluable to your customers—and will have customers begging to give you their business.
- The secrets of change psychology that will enable you to become a highly effective change agent and an important asset for your customers.

Before we look at how selling change is different from traditional solution and strategy sales approaches, let's further explore why change is a matter of survival.

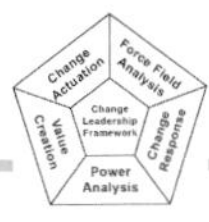






## Four Forces Changing Your World

While there are always innumerable forces driving change, four forces in particular are now changing the world you live in and are threatening your survival as a salesperson, the survival of the companies for whom you work, and the survival of the companies and people to whom you sell.

### 1. The Flat World

As you probably know all too well, you are now competing on a level playing field that extends to the four corners of the earth. In his book, *The World is Flat*, Pulitzer Prize-winning journalist Thomas Friedman documented ten forces that have flattened the world, giving equal opportunity to people around the world to compete for the same business. He calls this evolution, "Globalization 3.0," where individuals, not companies (Globalization 2.0) or countries (Globalization 1.0), must compete against other individuals on the other side of the world for the same opportunities.

The critical implication of a flat world is that all competitors must match the prices of the competitor who achieves the lowest cost, thereby flattening pricing across the competitive landscape and creating a Darwinian environment for improving efficiencies.

The critical implication of Globalization 3.0 is that *you* must personally match the wages of the competitor who can do what you do at the lowest cost. The same applies to your customers.

Friedman notes another implication of Globalization 3.0—"The Death of a Salesman." The biggest competition for your job as a salesperson is not another salesperson in another country—it is the Internet. Friedman notes that the Internet gives buyers unprecedented power to get the best business terms without the involvement of a salesperson, greatly reducing if not eliminating the traditional role of salespeople to inform and transact a purchase. Friedman reports, "'It's like they [customers] have cut all the fat [salespeople] out of the business and turned it into a numbers game."

## 2. Virtual Integration

Authors such as Alvin Toffler, Charles Handy, Geoffrey Moore, and others have forecasted the trend of companies to rely increasingly on other companies and individuals to perform important tasks. In the past, companies strove to integrate all aspects of their business into their internal operations with the intent of controlling costs and market dynamics. For example, IBM used to design and manufacture all the components of a computer, assemble the computer system, write the software, sell both the computer and software directly to the customer, and provide professional services and support. Today, a Chinese company, Lenovo, makes and sells the computers and IBM provides the technical support to Lenovo's customers. Why? Lenovo can make computers profitably at lower margins, while IBM can focus on providing the best professional services at higher margins. In fact, IBM has made such an effort to create a loosely coupled organizational structure that the current joke among IBM employees is that IBM stands for "I'm By Myself." What a dramatic change from the top-down, command-and-control, integrate-everything approaches of the past!

Geoffrey Moore calls this strategy "outsourcing context" and "in-sourcing core." He says, "A task is 'core' when it directly affects the competitive advantage of the company in its targeted markets. This is the ground upon which companies differentiate, and the goal of core work is to create and sustain that differentiation." Any task that does not create differentiation for a company is "context."

Moore argues companies maximize value for their shareholders by focusing solely on core activities and outsourcing all others. In other words, if you cannot perform the task better than everyone else, you should hire the people who do it better. Of course, this notion is not new—Adam Smith described the efficiencies of dividing labor in *The Wealth of Nations* published in 1776. What is new is a world flattened by technology, namely the Internet; a world in which the most efficient source of a task is a mouse click away.

The drive toward virtually integrated companies presents two challenges that salespeople can address: (a) companies become

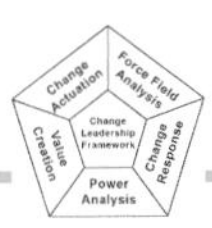




increasingly interdependent and (b) companies must not only optimize their own differentiating tasks, but they must also optimize across company boundaries. The result is a reframing of company relationships from "buyer-seller," (i.e., "Give me the best price, and I don't care if you lose money on every unit.") to "partner-partner," (i.e., "Let's work collaboratively to create the most differentiation.") The most successful salespeople will adapt their role to provide value in these increasingly collaborative relationships.

### 3. Future Shock

In his 1970 book, *Future Shock*, Alvin Toffler forecasted a world in which change would happen so fast that it would exceed people's ability to keep up. Have you ever bought a computer or a cell phone, only to realize a month later that a better, cheaper model is now available? You didn't even have time to pay the credit card bill or learn all the features before the model became "old." That is an example of future shock.

Toffler argued the increasing pace of change enabled by technology would eliminate the concept of "permanent," as in "permanent" employment or "permanent" occupation. He proposed that every aspect of life would not only be temporary, it would be transient—constantly in the process of moving from one state to another. He suggested people would have to learn new occupations not just once in their lives, but several times. Those people not willing or able to make changes would be shocked by their newly found poverty. Charles Handy, the author of *The Age of Unreason*, went a step further suggesting people would need to have "portfolios" of occupations and "portfolios" of employers.

Evidence of the increasing rate of change and of the implications forecasted by Toffler and Handy abound. The saying, "the only constant is change," may not be true after all. Change is not constant—it is increasing.

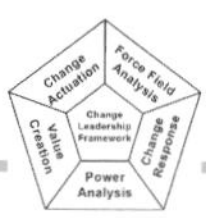


## 4. The Great Reboot of 2009

The state of the worldwide economy in 2009 may be remembered as the "Great Reboot." Economists and historians will undoubtedly fill entire libraries analyzing the causes of the biggest economic downturn since the Great Depression. But, one thing became clear during the economic events of 2009—many companies' finances were not as rosy as they had been portrayed. Over the previous decades in the drive to meet "Wall Street expectations" companies did everything possible—and impossible—to squeeze another x percent growth from the proverbial turnip. The economic environment of 2009 revealed weak business practices, balance sheets, productivity improvement, and actual customer demand that had all been masked previously.

Now, as the economy turns around and companies regain their footing, companies are going through radical transformations, or disappearing altogether. Lehman Brothers, a 125 year-old company that had survived the Great Depression, disappeared in a matter of months. Companies are "right-sizing" for actual demand, divesting unproductive assets, eliminating inefficiencies, and resetting "Wall Street expectations." It is as if all the bad baggage had been accumulating until finally the worldwide economy "crashed" like a computer displaying the blue-screen-of-death and a giant hand pressed the reset button. The economy is rebooting into a new, clean state that will run with renewed efficiency and reliability. The amount of change happening now will likely continue to ripple through the economy for the next decade.

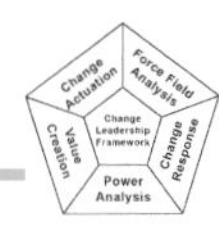




## Why Selling Change?

What do all of these forces that are changing the world in unprecedented ways with unprecedented speed have to do with you? Furthermore, what do they have to do with *Selling Change*?

Everything.

Change is everywhere. Change is everything. Those companies and salespeople who don't just adapt to change, but become the leaders of change, will be those who succeed in the new, flat, virtual, shocking, rebooted world.

So, how do you become a change leader? To be a change leader, you must, not surprisingly, change the way you sell. To better answer the question, let's compare the ways you have sold in the past to how you need to sell today.

The way you sell implies that you have certain capabilities, which can be described in a model called a capability maturity model. Let's examine the following maturity model, which applies both to you as a professional salesperson and to your sales organization as a whole.

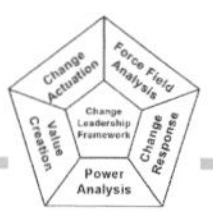


### *Sales Capability Maturity Model*

| Capabilities & Characteristics | Level 1 Transaction-Centric | Level 2 Solution-Centric | Level 3 Strategy-Centric | Level 4 Change-Centric |
|---|---|---|---|---|
| **Basis of competition** | Vendor price and delivery | Vendor features | Customer business benefits | Customer business strategy |
| **Knowledge areas** | Pricelist, fulfillment | Application of products and services in customer environment | Understanding customer business and personal motives | Understanding customer goals, environment, behaviors, and strategies |
| **Key profitability metrics** | Transaction velocity | Margins | Premium pricing | Lifetime Value |
| **Selling basis** | Mapping products or services to needs | Mapping product or service as a solution to problems | Mapping solutions to business strategy | Mapping business strategy to change strategy |
| **Value proposition** | Savings | Return on investment | Business value | Strategic value |
| **Level of engagement** | Purchasing agent | Project manager | Middle management | Executive management |
| **Number of competitors and substitutes** | Many | Several | Two or three | None |

## Level 1 (Transaction-Centric)

A level-one salesperson or organization focuses on transaction velocity, competing primarily on price and delivery. In a transaction-centric sale, the customer seeks to fulfill a well-defined need with a well-defined product or service and simply wants the best price and delivery terms. The key value proposition is savings—money or time. The buyer is typically a purchasing agent or other administrator who, like the level-one salesperson, also focuses on transaction velocity and efficiency.

## Level 2 (Solution-Centric)

The solution-centric salesperson is an expert in the product's features and how to apply them in the customer's environment to solve certain problems. If the salesperson is successful in demon-

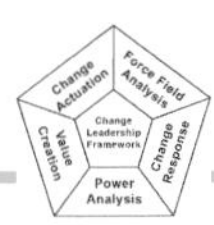




strating how the company's products and services solve the problems better than other options, then she will win the business and achieve higher margins. Therefore, her management measures not only her revenue, but the margins of her deals. The salesperson justifies deals to the customer at higher margins by showing the customer how he will enjoy an attractive return on investment, even at the higher price. Because this argument doesn't work very well with purchasing agents who are only focused on price and delivery, the salesperson must be able to gain access to the managers whose business will benefit from the purchase.



**Level 3 (Strategy-Centric)**

The strategic salesperson takes the benefits of purchasing the products and services to the next level. This salesperson shows how the products and services not only solve problems but how they align with the customer's business strategy. This requires a deep understanding of the customer's business, as well as knowledge of the customer's personal motives and benefits. The salesperson is able to garner premiums because she has demonstrated that not only will the benefits of the product exceed the cost, but they will enable the customer's strategies.

Although the salesperson may work with someone assigned to the project of acquiring a solution, she is able to take the value proposition to the next level—to the managers responsible for implementing the business strategies. These managers are more concerned about the success of the business strategies and reducing risks than they are about reducing costs. Because the salesperson is able to demonstrate the business value to the business managers, she makes the "short-list" of vendors and her proposal is one of the three proposals the company's purchasing policies require the manager to evaluate.

**Level 4 (Change-Centric)**

A level-four salesperson sees business strategy as a way to make a change—a way to get from here to there, a way to achieve the goals of the person or organization. She knows that having a

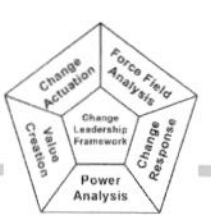


winning strategy is only half the challenge for the customer—effective strategy requires effective change.

Important strategies often require changes in the organization, such as changes in processes, people, or technology—and people naturally resist changes. Therefore, a critical capability of the change-centric salesperson is the ability to gain a deep understanding of the customer's goals, environment, culture, behavior, and strategies. With this understanding, the salesperson assists the customer in mapping the business strategy to the change strategy. To do this the level-four salesperson must have access to, and the trust of, the executives who define the strategy and direct its implementation.

The value proposition of the change-centric salesperson is that by buying from her company, the customer will be able to accomplish the changes the strategy is intended to achieve. Because few, if any, other vendors are able to make this proposition, the competition is not in serious contention for the business and the salesperson does not have to compete on price. In fact, the customer wants to make sure the deal is profitable and her company is financially sound because the customer is relying on her company to deliver. The salesperson and her company have a trusted, long-term relationship with the customer, so her management has the luxury of being able to look beyond current fiscal periods to measure and maximize the total anticipated value of the business over the lifetime of the relationship with the customer (Lifetime Value).

### Yesterday versus Today

Differentiating based on price-and-delivery, solutions, or even business strategy, worked well in the past. But, to win in the new rapidly changing world of today, you will need to lead change. You will need to become change-centric.

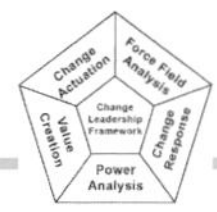






## Why Change?

- Are you making as much money as you can?
- Are you overachieving your revenue goals?
- Are you locking out competition from your customer accounts?
- Are you immune to pricing pressures in your business?
- Are you growing your business as quickly as you like?
- Are you able to keep your business on the same path because there are no changes in your business and the market conditions are very stable?
- Are you achieving everything you want in your life?

If any of the answers are no, then *Selling Change* will help you:

- Increase your revenue and income
- Lock out your competitors
- Maintain higher profit margins
- Improve the competitiveness of your sales force
- Become a strategic resource for your clients
- Have buyers calling you instead of you calling buyers
- Improve your order pipeline and forecasting
- Develop strong, long-term relationships with your customers
- Bust the myth that salespeople have to be pushy to be successful
- Achieve your financial and personal goals

We all wish we could make events change like Dr. Who traveling through time (from the British TV show), and we wish we could make people move instantly from one place to another like the Transporter in *Star Trek*. But, whether we like it or not, the reality is that we live in a Newtonian world where bodies at rest stay at rest unless a force is applied, and bodies in motion stay in motion unless another force is applied. So if we want to influence those bodies, we need to get very good at understanding the forces that are being exerted on them. Applying this reality to your business and your life means if you want to influence your customers, influence your organization, influence the people in your life, and influence your life in general, you need to be a master at understanding and harnessing the forces that are influencing

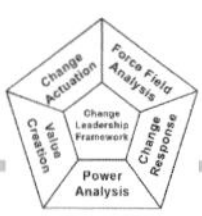


those situations. That leads to Secret # 3, which we will discuss in the next section.

But first, let's look at what happens if you do not embrace the forces of change to become a leader rather than a follower. Those organizations that do not operate as leaders will be subject to ever-increasing competition. They will need to scale back their cost structures dramatically to live on razor-thin margins and, on a personal level, scale back their personal lifestyles to live on a fraction of their disposable income.

If such downsizing does not sound very palatable, organizations can choose to become change leaders, driving high-value change on behalf of their customers, and thereby, not just maintaining their revenues and margins, but growing them. Not only will their businesses continue to grow, but they will build more and more sustainable competitive advantage, because those organizations that choose to live on razor-thin margins will fall farther and farther behind without the resources to catch up.

But this is not just a decision of the CEO or the board of directors. The first decision lies with you. You are the CEO of "Me Incorporated," and you are subject to the same dynamics, albeit on a personal scale. There are two kinds of people who will read this book.

The first kind of person will read this book and say, "Okay, I hear what you are saying, but you are asking me to change. You are asking me to change the way I think and the way I operate. I don't have time for that right now. I have a huge number of problems I deal with every day, and I'm doing everything I can just to keep up with everything that is going on. Maybe, once things calm down a little, I can think about how I might make some changes." Those people will continue to see their revenues and profits erode.

The second kind of person will say, "Forget that! I'm going to be a change leader, not a change victim. I'm going to get ahead and stay ahead of change." Those people will avail themselves of new opportunities and reap new rewards. They will maintain and

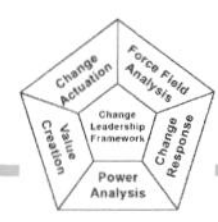






enhance their margins and their lifestyles. They will get farther and farther ahead of their competitors. Eventually, they will be so far ahead people will complain, "It's not fair." Now, ask yourself, "Do I want to be the one complaining, or the one leading?"

### How to Read This Book

*Selling Change* is designed as a handbook (ribbon bookmarker; no dust jacket) to be kept at your side for real-time, on-the-go, insight and inspiration. It contains 107 "secrets", or principles, of effective change leadership. Each principle is concisely written as What I Need to Know and What I Need to Do to put the principle in action. Because the principles are easy to read, you may be tempted to read quickly through the entire book. If you take this approach, you'll want to (a) look for the key ideas that presently strike a chord and (b) strive to understand the overall Change Leadership Framework.

However, each "secret" actually summarizes complex ideas about which entire books have been written. So, you can read this book over and over, gaining new insights each time. I highly recommend you keep this book handy and read a secret every morning. After reading the secret ask yourself three questions:

1. Have I seen instances of this idea in my business or life?
2. How might I have applied this principle and how might it have affected the outcome?
3. How can I apply this principle, today?

### Goal

The goal of this book is to help you grow and then maintain a change-centric view of your customers, of people and organizations, and of your own life—to view them as a set of forces and a set of changes. I guarantee that when you take a change-centric view and learn to harness the forces of change, you will experience explosive growth, both in your sales and in your life.

This is probably the time to let you in on secret # 1.

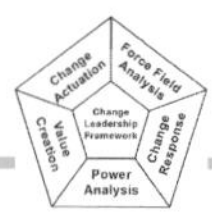


# SECRET # 1
# THE WORLD IS CHANGING

*The world is moving so fast these days that the man who says it can't be done is generally interrupted by someone doing it.*
*—Elbert Hubbard*

## WHAT I NEED TO KNOW

Okay, the fact that the world is changing is not much of a secret, especially if you read the preceding introduction. Change stares you in the face every day, whether you are shaving new beard growth or putting on makeup. But many people overlook change, ignore it, or deny it. Unless you embrace change and lead it, you are going to get steamrolled by it. You are going to wake up one day, look in the mirror, and realize the world has passed by.

In the world of sales not so long ago, it used to be that buyers would look for solutions from local representatives. Those sellers with the ability to build relationships, understand the buyer's problem, and position their products and services as the best solution to that problem, could win the business.

**Internet Empowerment.** Now, approaching two decades after the birth of the World Wide Web, buyers are increasingly able to tap into the wealth of information on the Internet and educate themselves, both on defining the problem and on finding the best solution.

**Globalization.** To compound the power of the buyer, modern communication infrastructure provides superfast, always-on connections to vendors all over the world, who offer many advantages to buyers, including access to 24/7 workforces, lowest labor costs, and highest quality.

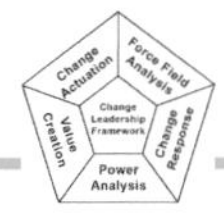



## What I Need to Do

The secret that will take your sales to new levels is making change a part of everything you do, see, feel, touch, and think—in other words, becoming change-centric.

Sales professionals and the companies they represent are faced with two choices: either become commoditized by global competition and Internet commerce, or significantly increase the value they add to the buyer.

Providing a solution to a problem is no longer sufficient to win the business. The professional salesperson must deeply understand the buyer's organizational challenges and become an agent of change, driving permanent business results for the customer.



## Action Summary

- Be in forward motion and always be changing.
- Eat change. Sleep change. Breathe change. Make your life all about change.

***Internet Empowerment***

***Globalization***

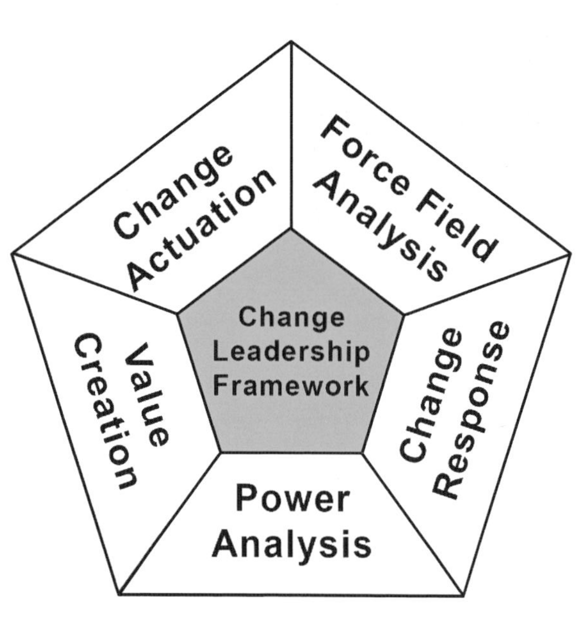
Change Actuation
Force Field Analysis
Change Leadership Framework
Value Creation
Change Response
Power Analysis

# CHANGE LEADERSHIP FRAMEWORK

## UNDERSTANDING THE PREMISES

# INTRODUCTION

# TO

# CHANGE LEADERSHIP FRAMEWORK PREMISES

## What is it?

The Change Leadership Framework is a way of thinking about and leading change. It operates on the premise that salespeople create the most value when they help customers achieve their goals.

## Why is it important?

What causes people to change?

How do people decide to change?

How do people make change?

To lead change, you must study the answers to these questions, which I call the "psychology of change." To implement your learning in practice, it is often helpful to organize the disparate concepts in a "framework." Frameworks make the concepts easier to understand and remember, and they serve as a kind of recipe for acting on the concepts. Therefore, in my previous book, *Forceful Selling*, I introduced the Change Leadership Framework® to capture key concepts in the psychology of change and to describe a process for leading change in people and organizations.

## How is it new or different?

This change-centric approach, which applies concepts of change psychology to the selling process, is an important evolution in selling theory. Over the last 20 years top sales professionals have been taught to uncover the customer's problem, define a solution, and discover the benefits of solving the problem—a reactive process that, today, occurs more and more frequently over the Internet, thereby devaluing the role of the salesperson. To preserve their value and prevent their company's products from becoming low-margin commodities, salespeople must proactively create value by leading the changes necessary to unlock customer value.

## What are the common misconceptions?

A common myth is that successful salespeople and change leaders must behave like ravenous bulldogs, aggressively biting onto opportunities, and pursuing them furiously until the customer relents. While tenacity and perseverance are qualities that help change leaders achieve the customer's desired outcomes, pushy salespeople will not make strong change-centric salespeople. Therefore, a bulldog character, Joe Bulldog (affectionately referred to as J.B.), is used in the illustrations throughout this book to parody the myth of the bulldog salesperson and to illustrate the core concept in each secret.

## What are the key take-aways & how do I put them in action?

To avoid being replaced by a web page, or seeing your margins and commissions squeezed paper-thin, you need to become an agent of change that helps your customers achieve their goals rather than simply solve their problems. Start by asking, "What is your goal?" instead of asking, "What is your problem?"

When you help customers achieve their goals, you become invaluable to them and your sales and profits will soar.

# SECRET # 2
# PEOPLE ONLY BUY WHEN FORCED

*A man would rather have a hole in his head than a hole in his pocket and lose a dollar.*

*—Brett Clay*

## WHAT I NEED TO KNOW

When is the last time you took a hundred dollar bill, put a match to it and said, "Ahhh. That felt good"? For most people, that is not a pleasant thought. They know and feel how much work that hundred dollars represents. They know how far and how long they can drive on one hundred dollars' worth of gas. They know how much of that one hundred dollars is left after buying a week's worth of groceries. Or should I say they know how many days worth of groceries a hundred dollars will buy? So, almost any person would rather have a hole in his head than lose one hundred dollars.

When someone gives a hundred dollar bill to someone, he is not doing it for fun; he is doing so because something is forcing him. As a salesperson, I sold multimillion-dollar software applications and multimillion-dollar supercomputers so I can tell you that the last thing the vice presidents who signed those purchase orders wanted to do was sign a multimillion-dollar purchase order. They did so only because they felt like aristocrats in the French Revolution and they did not want to see their heads on a pole. If it weren't for the fact that the use of my company's product could determine the success or failure of the customer's entire company, the vice presidents would have rather seen a freight train coming at them than me coming toward them with a multimillion-dollar quotation.

## What I Need to Do

Have empathy and compassion for your customers. Put yourself in their positions and realize how difficult the purchase decision is.

Seek to understand the forces that are driving a possible purchase and help the customer to evaluate them.

The role of a change leader is much like that of a counselor. Help the customer cope with the forces and evaluate his options for responding to them by asking counseling questions like:

- How do you feel about that?
- What options have you explored?
- Have you considered [other options]?
- What factors do you feel are most important in your decision?
- When must you take action?

These questions help the customer decide how to respond to the force he feels.



## Action Summary

- Be empathetic—put yourself in the customer's shoes.
- Understand what is forcing the customer to take action.
- Be a counselor—ask probing questions.

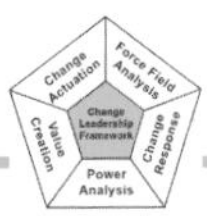

# Secret # 3
# You Are Not a Force

*Pull the string and it will follow wherever you wish. Push it, and it will go nowhere at all.*

*—Dwight D. Eisenhower*

## What I Need to Know

While it is true that people buy because they are forced to buy, it is not true they can be forced by you!

You cannot force people to buy. Period.

First, people have an extreme dislike for pushy salespeople. If people feel they are being pushed or forced, their emotions will take over, and they will resist buying, even if it hurts them not to.

Second, it is a waste of your time, energy, and resources to push people. Pushing people who are not motivated is like trying to carry a horse to the trough—extremely arduous and bordering on impossible. You will be far more successful, and much less frustrated, if you let the customer push. That is like jumping on a hungry horse's back when the bell rings at feeding time. You can only go where the horse wants to go, which is to the grain bin, but you will get there really fast!

Third, if the customer feels you are trying to force a purchase, the customer will not trust that you are working in their best interests.

Change leadership is counterintuitive in that the change leader must lead where the followers want to go. That is why the concept of a change "agent" is more appropriate, that is, a person employed by the customer to achieve the customer's desire.

## WHAT I NEED TO DO

Let the "horse" decide where to go and when to go.

Calibrate your mindset that you are the customer's agent, the customer's servant, looking out for your master's best interest.

See yourself as a service provider. The service you provide is to assist the customer in making a change and achieving her desired outcome. Your product or service is just the vehicle for the change and the desired outcome.

When the customer takes action to make a purchase and make a change, it will be because something forced him to do so. Seek to understand what that will be.



## ACTION SUMMARY

- Do NOT try to force people.
- Do NOT even consider yourself part of the equation.
- Do be an agent who can be trusted to help the customer.

# Secret # 4
# No One Needs Your Product

*He that is good with a hammer tends to think everything is a nail.*

*—Abraham Maslow*

## What I Need to Know

Do people buy your product because they need it?

All sales courses teach the fundamental concept of "need satisfaction selling." The notion is that people buy things in order to satisfy a need or want, to fill a gap, to solve a problem. While the concept seems straightforward, there is a subtle but incredibly powerful point about buying that even the brightest people often do not understand. That is, the customer's problem is not that he does not own your product. His need is not your product. Rather, your product satisfies a need perceived by your customer.

I have worked with genius-level Ph.D.s from Cambridge University in England, Harvard M.B.A.s with many years in marketing at name-brand consumer products companies, engineers who truly believe that customers will come running for their better mousetrap, and salespeople with many years of sales experience. In every case, when I asked them, "What is the customer's problem? What does the customer need?" they said, "His problem is that he needs my product."

Okay, let's try this again. Let's say you need to obtain your management's approval to purchase a widget. When you ask your manager to sign the purchase requisition, your manager asks, "Why do we need this?" You say, "Because we don't have it." Is it likely your manager will say, "Oh. Okay. Then, here's my approval"? Absolutely not!

## What I Need to Do

Get over it. People need to stay alive. People need to satisfy their hunger. People need their problems solved. But people don't need your product!

The customer's problem is not that he does not own your product. So, find out what the real problem is. But more important, find out what the customer is trying to accomplish. The customer was likely trying to do something and then ran into an obstacle. That obstacle became the "problem." Add more value, not just by addressing the obstacle, but by helping the customer accomplish the goal.

And don't stop there. Find out why the goal exists. What is the need the customer is trying to satisfy by achieving the goal? That is what the customer "needs."



## Action Summary

- Look for the customer's problem.
- Look for the goal the problem is inhibiting.
- Look for the need the goal is satisfying.

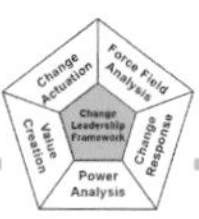


# SECRET # 5
# PEOPLE BUY TO MAKE A CHANGE

*To be a success in business, be daring, be first, be different.*
*—Henry Marchant*

## WHAT I NEED TO KNOW

Now that you know one of the most important secrets—that people do not buy products because they need them—they buy products to satisfy a need, the question becomes "Why does the person have a need?"

We will discuss needs in more detail later in the book, but for now, we will say a need or problem arises from a person's desire to make a change.

Think of some of your recent purchases. First, there are the trivial examples such as grocery purchases. You "needed" those groceries because you wanted to change your ability to eat at home. Without food in the refrigerator, you would have to eat at a restaurant outside your home or go hungry. So, what forces you to eat at home? Apparently, you wanted to make another change. Perhaps you wanted to change your health by avoiding unhealthy fast foods. Perhaps you wanted to change your ability to add money to your savings account, assuming you could eat at home for less money.

A less trivial personal example is the purchase of a car. If you traded in your old car to buy a newer one, you were making a change, both literally and in your mind. What were you trying to change by buying a different car? Were you trying to change the reliability of your transportation? Were you changing the size of your family? Were you changing your image? What was changing?

## WHAT I NEED TO DO

Look beyond the "need." Look for what is changing.

Some products and services may not appear to be associated with changes. When you go to the grocery store week after week, it might seem that nothing is changing. You simply "need" food. But could you really eat the same thing for breakfast, lunch, and dinner, day after day?

It is true that some products and services involve less change than others. But your ability to continue winning the orders week after week depends on your ability to find or create change. If you don't, then someone else will do it to you. For example, is there a restaurant in your town that has taken a very common, unchanging item, such as the hamburger, and made some changes that result in your willingness to pay a lot of money for it? Perhaps it has special meat, or special condiments. Or perhaps the restaurant is decorated like a gold mine or a barn.

As a change leader, you must find or create a change beyond the apparent "need."



## ACTION SUMMARY

- Look beyond the need—look for the changes driving the need.
- Create a "change experience" for your customer.
- Be the first to change—before your competitor does!

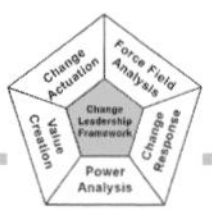


# SECRET # 6
# PROBLEMS ARE THE TIP OF THE ICEBERG

*Some people see problems and solutions.*
*I see changes and destinations.*
*—Brett Clay*

## WHAT I NEED TO KNOW

Understanding the customer's problem is really important. As salespeople, we often have a solution looking for a problem. Our job is often to find someone who has the problem that can be solved by our product.

However, problems and solutions are just the tip of the iceberg. Under the surface are all of the forces and changes acting on the organization. When an organization responds to the forces acting on it by making a change, a problem "surfaces." The problem on the surface is merely a symptom of the forces acting under the surface.

For every problem recognized by an organization and for every solution vendors offer to solve the problem, there are many forces at work in the organization. It is common for customers to be well down the path looking for a specific solution when they have not adequately defined the problem, let alone thoroughly assessed the underlying situation.

You will be valued far more by the customer if you assist in addressing the underlying issues. You will also find a much bigger set of opportunities under the surface.

## WHAT I NEED TO DO

Look for the problems and solutions. But then look underneath the surface.

Ask the following questions, using terms the customer is familiar with:

- What is changing?
- What is the destination that the customer is trying to reach?
- What are the forces at play?
- In what direction are the forces pointing?
- How will the forces play out?

If the customer is confronted by an urgent and critical problem, she may only be willing to discuss immediate solutions to bandage the problem quickly. Pick the appropriate time to probe under the surface and discover the underlying causes. You will likely build your understanding of the forces acting on the organization over time. The key is to have a mindset of looking for forces and changes rather than merely looking for problems.



## ACTION SUMMARY

- Listen to the customer's description of the problem and the ideal solution.
- Discover the forces and changes happening under the surface.
- Address underlying issues to identify bigger opportunities, deliver more value, and grow your revenues.

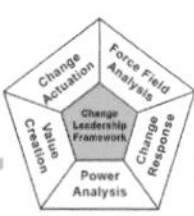

# Secret # 7
# Delivery Trumps Relationship

*The ultimate delivery is customer success;*
*the ultimate price is failure.*

*—Brett Clay*

## What I Need to Know

Have you heard the saying, "Buyers buy from people they like"? You will find that statement in every sales book ever written. But is it true? Is sales all about being the smooth-talking, back-slapping personality who is the life of the party?

Well, here is a new saying for you, "Buyers buy from websites they like."

If it has not happened already, your customer is about to break up with you and start having a relationship with a website. What can a salesperson do, other than sit by the phone and eat comfort food? Deliver!

Today's Internet-savvy buyers do not buy based on personality and relationships. They buy based on price and delivery. Competing on price is a losing proposition because someone on the Internet will always be offering your product and service at a lower price—probably for free. That's the allure of the Internet. Your only option is to focus on delivery—delivering the customer's desired result with the highest quality and lowest risk. In other words, deliver customer success.

Salespeople who develop trust by consistently delivering customer success will have the most valuable long-term clients and the biggest revenue growth.

## What I Need to Do

Forget about competing on "relationship." Your relationship is not as compelling to the customer as getting the best price and quality from the Internet.

Forget about competing on price. You'll never make money and you'll never build a base of loyal, satisfied customers.

Focus on delivering customer success, that is, achieving the customer's desired result with the highest quality and lowest risk.

Delivery = Trust. By consistently delivering customer success, you become a trusted resource for the buyer.

Trust = Revenue. Once you are a trusted resource, the orders will go to you instead of your competitor.



## Action Summary

- Deliver customer success.
- Do not compromise quality or risk.
- Focus more on building trust than on building the relationship.

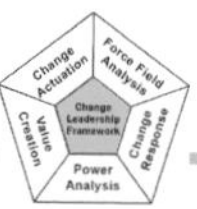

# Secret # 8
# Opportunity Only Comes with Change

*He who rejects change is the architect of decay. The only human institution that rejects progress is the cemetery.*
*—Edmund Wilson*

## What I Need to Know

I will use two analogies: a sailboat and a brick road.

Leaks in a sailboat, torn sails, and broken winches are all examples of problems. Solving those problems keeps the boat afloat. But having a boat that floats does not mean it is going to go anywhere. Only by making changes, such as setting the sails and tacking back and forth, will the boat sail to a destination.

Problems are also like bricks in the road—they are finite and the number of problems just keeps going and going, as far as the eye can see. Sometimes the problems seem more like boulders or mountains than bricks. But in all cases, they are on the path to where you want to go. In *The Wonderful Wizard of Oz* by L. Frank Baum, Dorothy is told to follow the yellow brick road to reach the Emerald City where she will find the Wizard of Oz. Her visit with the Wizard in Emerald City is a milestone in her journey to return to her home in Kansas.

Likewise, problems are bricks in the road that form a path to reach milestones in your business and in your life. Changes are the milestones in your journey. Changes are the destinations you try to reach through solving problems.

We often get caught up in the problems and lose the perspective that the problems are just bricks. Only by achieving changes will we open opportunities and reach our goals.

## What I Need to Do

Before you leave work for the day, or before you go to sleep at the end of the day, ask yourself, "What did I change today?" If you did not change anything, you did not create any opportunities.

Then, before you go to sleep, ask yourself, "What am I going to change tomorrow?" If you only make one small change every day, then when you look back at the end of the year, you will have accomplished far more than you could have imagined.

After you experience the power of change, you will become passionate and want to help others experience the benefits. When you passionately believe in the power of change, as can only happen through experiencing it, you will glow with enthusiasm, confidence, and substance. Your passion will be infectious and you will successfully help your customers create new opportunities and enjoy new rewards.



## Action Summary

- Make one change per day.
- Seek new opportunities for yourself and your customers.
- Count your blessings; then count your changes.

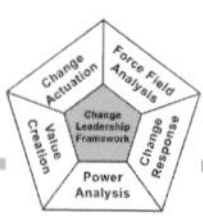


# SECRET # 9
# BECOME A CHANGE LEADER

*Leadership is action, not position.*
*—Donald H. McGannon*

## WHAT I NEED TO KNOW

Change-centric selling changes the sales paradigm from asking middle managers, "What is your problem?" to asking executives, "What are you trying to change? Why? How?"

The change-centric selling model takes the following approach:

1. **Mining opportunities**
    - Create, rather than respond to opportunities
    - Focus on deeper relationships with fewer customers
2. **Developing strategic value**
    - Understand the forces affecting the customer
    - Help define and drive strategic changes on behalf of the customer
3. **Maintaining lifetime relationships**
    - Become a change consultant and agent
    - Evolve with the customer's evolving capability maturity

## What I Need to Do

The first step is to help the customer identify opportunities. Remember that opportunities are created by making changes.

Next, seek to understand the forces influencing the customer's organization and that organization's ability to implement changes.

Then, help the customer define what changes she wants to make in response to the forces.

Be a change consultant and agent by assisting the customer in achieving the desired changes.

Finally, maintain a lifetime relationship with the customer by continuing to identify opportunities and assisting the customer in continuously evolving her capability to exploit them.



## Action Summary

- Help customers identify opportunities to change.
- See yourself as a change consultant.
- Maintain your value by continuously evolving your own capabilities.

# SECRET # 10
# THE CHANGE LEADERSHIP FRAMEWORK®

*So with imagination, ingenuity, and audacity, explore, discover, and change the world.*

*—Daniel S. Goldin*

## WHAT I NEED TO KNOW

If change-centric selling is essentially about helping the customer achieve change, how does the salesperson go about it? The answer is the Change Leadership Framework, which is comprised of five disciplines:

1. **Force Field Analysis**
   - What forces is the person experiencing?
2. **Change Response Analysis**
   - How will the person respond to the forces?
3. **Power Analysis**
   - What effort will be required to make the desired change?
4. **Value Creation**
   - What will be the value of making the change?
5. **Change Actuation**
   - How will the change be made?

By utilizing the Change Leadership Framework as a blueprint for helping customers achieve their desired results, you will not only be an outstanding change leader, but you will become a highly valued resource for your customers, putting you in the best position to succeed in a highly competitive world.

## What I Need to Do

Adeptly implement the Change Leadership Framework to help your customers achieve their desired results.

Improve your skill and comfort level by reviewing one concept from *Forceful Selling* or *Selling Change* every day and implementing it at least once during that day.

Some account relationships can be quite complex with many sales in different stages. Therefore, it may not be appropriate to impose a one-size-fits-all order on your activities. As you become more familiar with the concepts of change-centric selling, they will become tools you can pull out of your toolbox at the appropriate time.

The key is to maintain your focus on change and maintain your mindset as a change agent. Then, you will be able to establish and maintain your position as a strategic resource for your customer.



## Action Summary

- Read one secret of change leadership every day.
- Improve your change leadership by practicing a new concept every day.
- Drive continuous incremental improvement—both on behalf of the customer and in your own activities.

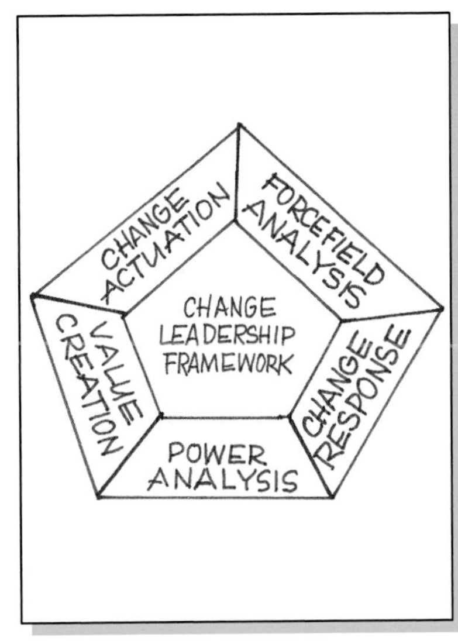

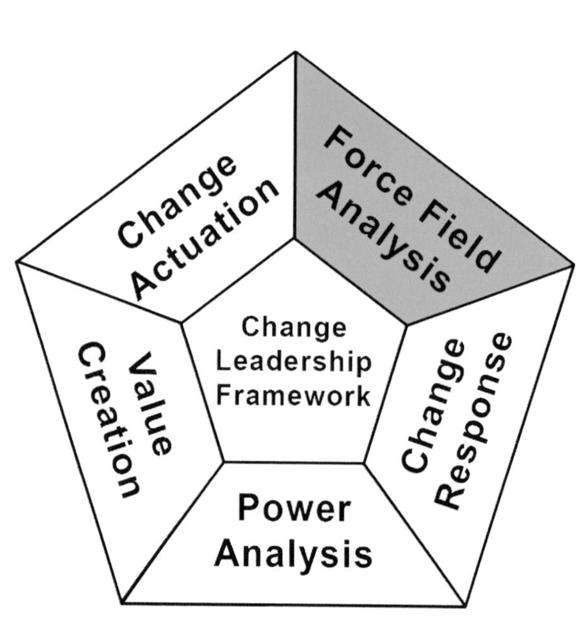
Change Actuation
Force Field Analysis
Change Leadership Framework
Value Creation
Change Response
Power Analysis

# FORCE FIELD ANALYSIS

## THE FIRST DISCIPLINE

# INTRODUCTION

# TO

# FORCE FIELD ANALYSIS

## What is it?

Force field analysis is the process of understanding the forces that the customer is feeling. In other words, What is driving the customer?

For 21st century readers, who may associate force fields with electromagnetic shields, tractor beams, and other science-fiction concepts, there may be some confusion about what a force field is. When German psychologist Kurt Lewin first introduced the term "force field" in the 1930's, he meant "a field of forces" (think of a field of flowers) where a force is tendency to move or change position. So force field analysis is the process of analyzing the interplay of forces and the resulting changes. Or simply put, it is the process of analyzing what drives people to take action.

The underlying principle of Lewin's theories and equations is that people and organizations make changes in response to forces they experience. Extending this principle to the study of buying behaviors results in the formation of several profoundly important selling principles, which I described in *Forceful Selling*. People and organizations make:

1. Purchases in order to effect change.
2. Purchases in response to forces they experience.
3. Changes and purchases when they are forced to do so.

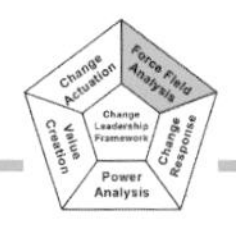




### Why is it important?

To best help the customer and have the best chance of closing a high-margin sale, you must understand what is driving the customer's actions and what the customer is trying to achieve.

### How is it new or different?

Salespeople have traditionally been taught to look for customers' pain and then suggest solutions. Solutions are like bandages. They heal a pain. But, are people satisfied simply by not being in pain? Or, do they actually want to feel good, to go somewhere, to get something accomplished? For example, are executives rewarded for keeping their company out of bankruptcy, or are they rewarded for growing the business and achieving investor goals? Changes and achievements are more valuable than problems and solutions.

### What are the common misconceptions?

One of the biggest mistakes I see salespeople and executives making is confusing problems with solutions. The English language is partly to blame. We say things like "I need a break," and "I need a coffee." But those are solutions not problems. A need is the existence of a problem, not the existence of a solution. But, there is an even more fundamental point here. Rather than asking, "Do you need a break?" ask, "Do you feel tired?" Focusing on what the customer feels is far more powerful and opens up a whole new world of possibilities for both the customer and the salesperson.

### What are the key take-aways & how do I put them in action?

You will be far more valued—and compensated—by your customers if you help them respond to the forces they feel and achieve their goals. Think of yourself as a counselor and ask customers what they feel.

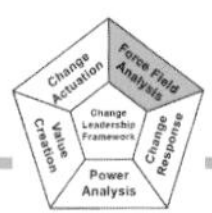


# SECRET # 11
# BE AN AMATEUR PSYCHOLOGIST

*Whatever you cannot understand, you cannot possess.*
*—Johann Wolfgang Von Goethe*

## WHAT I NEED TO KNOW

To be an effective change leader, you must have a deep understanding of the psychology of change.

Change is not easy. If it were easy, we all would have transformed ourselves into perfect beings. In fact, change is quite difficult. The difficulty lies in our ability to let go of the current situation and venture into a new, unknown situation. That process is the psychology of change.

An understanding of the psychology of change helps you find answers to the key questions that confront the change leader:

- What does the customer want to change?
- Why does the customer want to change?
- What does the customer really want? What is the customer's ultimate goal?
- What is preventing the customer from changing? Why has she not already changed?
- What motivates the customer? What makes the customer "tick"?
- What is involved in making the change? What will it take?
- How will the customer behave before, during, and after the change?

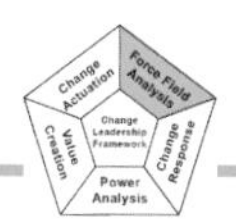



## WHAT I NEED TO DO

It is not necessary to be trained formally as a clinical psychologist. You do not have to be able to make diagnosis from the *DSM III*. But to be an outstanding change leader, you must be an earnest student of people's behavior and thinking. That is your remaining competitive edge over the Internet and your global competitors.

To gain more insight into the psychology of change, I recommend you read my book, *Forceful Selling*.

To gain more insight into how people think and behave, I recommend you read *Please Understand Me II* by David Keirsey. You will find Keirsey's descriptions of sixteen types of personalities very insightful and useful.

Do this exercise the next time you are in a public place: Look around the room and identify five different people. Ask yourself a number of the seven "W questions" for each, for example, Why is that person here? What was the first thing that person thought when he awoke this morning? Where does that person want to go in her life? What is the biggest change he will make this month?



## ACTION SUMMARY

- Be a student of people.
- Put yourself in their shoes.
- Develop an infinite curiosity and appreciation for people.

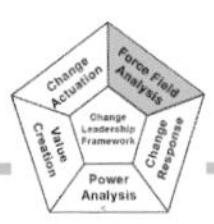


# SECRET # 12
# UNDERSTAND THE FOUR FORCES

*Success . . . means the opportunity to experience and to realize to the maximum the forces that are within us.*
*—David Sarnoff*

## WHAT I NEED TO KNOW

In *Principles of Topological Psychology*, Kurt Lewin proposed that behavior is a function of the person and his environment. The Change Leadership Framework® expands on Lewin's equation and models the forces that people and organizations experience on four dimensions, called the Four Forces:

1. **Internal needs**—<u>N</u>eeds
2. **Behavioral tendencies**—<u>B</u>ehaviors
3. **Cognitive strategies**—<u>S</u>trategies
4. **Environmental forces**—<u>E</u>nvironment

Therefore, the Change Leadership Framework proposes that Lewin's "person" (P) is a function of his internal (psychological) needs (N), his innate behavioral tendencies (B), and his cognitive strategies (S). Expressed as Lewin would have loved to have seen it, this concept would yield the equation, Behavior = f (N,B,S,E).

These four dimensions function as primary components that are exhaustively inclusive of the universe of forces acting on the person or organization. For example, while your computer can render up to 16.2 million different colors, they are all comprised of different amounts of just three colors—red, green, and blue. Similarly, while people may feel many different forces, the Change Leadership Framework models them on four primary dimensions: needs, behaviors, strategies, and environment.

## What I Need to Do

See people as a set of forces.

Develop the habit that every time you look at someone, you ask, "What forces does this person feel right now?"

Make profiles of the key stakeholders in your accounts and update them once a quarter. By definition, their behavioral tendencies should not change much over time, but their needs, strategies, and environment are constantly changing.

Constantly seek to develop a deeper understanding of your customers' force fields. For example, you might seek a deeper understanding of a customer's current emotional needs and how those needs have been met in the past. Every time you communicate with your customer, have a question prepared that improves your understanding.

Apply force field analysis to situations, as well, by identifying the factors that are influencing the situation. Then, seek to understand their sizes and how they will influence the final outcome.



## Action Summary

- Ask, "What forces is this person feeling, right now?"
- Constantly improve your knowledge of the customer.
- Apply force field analysis to all people and situations.

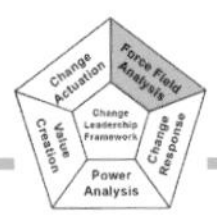


# SECRET # 13
# UNDERSTAND THE CLIENT'S INTERNAL NEEDS

*All progress is based on a universal innate desire on the part of every organism to live beyond its income.*

*—Samuel Butler*

## WHAT I NEED TO KNOW

The force at the core of everything we do is the force of our own needs and wants.

In his 1943 paper, titled "A Theory of Human Motivation," Abraham Maslow proposed a framework for explaining what motivates human behavior. Maslow theorized that "man is a perpetually wanting animal," and that once one need or want is satisfied, another will emerge. Furthermore, Maslow theorized that humans prioritize needs in a specific order or "hierarchy," whereby basic needs must be satisfied before the higher needs can exist.

Maslow's Hierarchy of Needs proposes a taxonomy of five classes:

- **Self-actualization**—the highest need; the need to be the most and happiest you can be
- **Esteem**—the desire for strength, achievement, recognition, and appreciation
- **Love and belonging**—the longing for social relationships
- **Safety**—the desire for safety and stability
- **Physiological**—the most basic need; the need to maintain bodily functions

While other theories of human motivation have also been proposed, what you really need to know is that people's internal needs, or motivations, are central to all of their activities and observed behaviors.

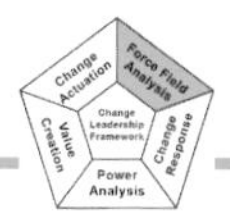




## What I Need to Do

Perhaps the most important task in change leadership is discovering the person or organization's internal needs—what they are ultimately striving to achieve. Try to understand the person or organization's:

- Status among Maslow's Hierarchy of Needs
- Motives
- Values
- Moods
- Goals
- Anxieties
- Ideals

All of these factors are "needs" that motivate human behavior. (Note: Don't confuse the noun "needs" as Maslow uses it, with the verb "to need" discussed in Secret # 4.) The better you understand how your customer is motivated and what he is trying to achieve, the better you will be able to help him achieve it.



## Action Summary

- Build an internal needs profile of the key stakeholders and decision makers in your accounts.
- Increase your understanding of the customer's needs over time.
- Remember: you are not selling a product—you are providing a service to help the customer satisfy her needs.

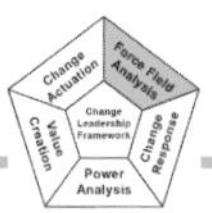


# Secret # 14
# Understand the Client's Behaviors

*Nothing worse could happen to one than to be completely understood.*

*—Carl Gustav Jung*

## What I Need to Know

Another powerful force that influences the behaviors of people and organizations is their behavioral tendencies. These behaviors are innate in the individual or the organization. In individuals, behavioral tendencies often are referred to as personality traits or temperament. In organizations, behavioral tendencies often are referred to as organizational culture.

In *Forceful Selling*, I defined a model called the Six Change Types, which coincidentally uses six factors, listed below, to assess people's ability and willingness to change, that is, their "change temperament." We'll discuss each of the change types (the animal metaphors depicted in the illustration on the opposite page) in more detail in Section 4, Change Response Analysis.

**Anxiety**. What kind of emotional "baggage" "hangs up" this person from adapting and changing effectively?

**Stability**. To what degree is the person prone to swings of emotion and neurotic behavior?

**Action**. Does the person have a high energy level and inclination for moving forward and solving problems?

**Confidence**. Is the person willing to venture into the unknown?

**Openness.** To what degree is the person receptive to new ideas and aware of multiple perspectives?

**Risk tolerance**. How much risk is the person willing to accept?

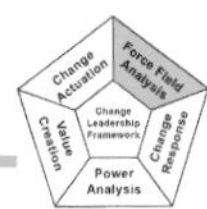




## What I Need to Do

Every person is different and every person's unique personality traits will form a unique set of forces that drive her behavior and how she changes. Assess each of your customers with the six factors to understand how their personalities influence their buying behaviors.

You likely already have an intuitive feel for your customers' personalities and their abilities to change. Use the six factors and the Six Change Types model to communicate clearly among your sales team the customer's characteristics in concrete terms.

Read *Please Understand Me II*, by David Keirsey for a thorough description of the sixteen personality types in his temperament model. Determine which temperament most closely matches your customer; then interact with the customer in the way most valued by that temperament.



## Action Summary

- Assess customers using the six factors (Six Change Types model).
- Determine customers' temperaments (Keirsey Temperament Sorter).
- Use these two models to predict customer behavior and desired changes.

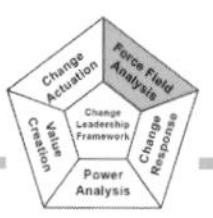


# SECRET # 15
# UNDERSTAND THE CLIENT'S STRATEGIES

*We are what we pretend to be, so we must be careful what we pretend to be.*

*—Kurt Vonnegut*

## WHAT I NEED TO KNOW

In the Change Leadership Framework the "strategy force" refers to the influence of the customer's cognitive processes, which are essentially the processes of thinking. Cognitive processes are very different from behavioral tendencies, because when you do something cognitively, you do it mindfully, thoughtfully, purposely; whereas behavioral tendencies are attitudes and actions that are automatic, mindless, and uncontrolled.

So, the third of the Four Forces that guide individual or organizational behavior and change is the "cognitive strategies" the person employs. In the scheme of the Change Leadership Framework, cognitive strategies are the overarching tools, techniques, plans, systems, and other cognitive processes the person routinely uses to satisfy internal needs and cope with environmental forces and behavioral tendencies.

It is important to note that "cognitive strategies," as used here, are not situation-specific strategies and tactics that plan a set of activities related to a certain situation. Rather, in the Change Leadership Framework, we are looking for the broad, cognitive strategies that act as guiding forces and influence the client's behavior.

The client's cognitive strategies may be the most important of the Four Forces because it is the only force the client can directly control.

## What I Need to Do

First, understand what strategies the customer is currently employing. These established systems may serve to support change, or in many cases, they may have become limitations themselves. You will need to decide whether it is more expeditious to lead change within the constraints of the customer's existing strategies or to change the strategies before leading the actual change initiative.

Second, develop new cognitive strategies to drive change. Remember, of the Four Forces, the customer has the most control over the strategies she employs. So, work with the customer to implement strategies that result in desired changes in the other three areas, that is, internal needs, behavioral tendencies, and environmental factors.



## Action Summary

- Understand how strategies are limiting forces.
- Leverage existing strategies to support change.
- Drive new strategies to effect change among the Four Forces.

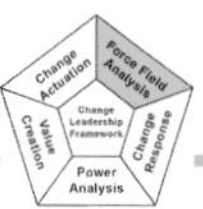


# SECRET # 16
# UNDERSTAND THE CLIENT'S ENVIRONMENT

*Circumstances are the rulers of the weak; they are but the instruments of the wise.*

*—Samuel Lover*

## WHAT I NEED TO KNOW

The last of the Four Forces in the Change Leadership Framework are the forces that are external to the person or organization.

We cannot be separated from our environment. Although we may, at times, attempt to separate ourselves mentally from our environment and explore the limits of our imagination, we still depend on our environment for our very existence. Various psychologists have additionally argued that without interactions and relationships with others, we would also perish. So the environment undoubtedly plays an enormous role in our lives.

The list of environmental forces is infinite, but here are some examples:

- Local societal influences
- Company culture and politics
- Family and friends
- Economy
- Competitors
- Technology

When people think of change, they usually think of changing their environment. But people must thoroughly analyze the environmental forces and then assess them in the context of the other three forces before an optimal change plan can be formulated.

## What I Need to Do

Being a highly effective change leader requires disciplined thoroughness. Be sure to analyze the customer's environmental forces as thoroughly as you analyze the forces of the customer's internal needs, behavioral tendencies, and cognitive strategies—and vice versa.

Depending on the nature of your product and service, a basic understanding of the key environmental forces that are influencing the current purchase may be sufficient. As the value of your product and service increases, however, a deep understanding of the environmental forces enables you to forecast trends and develop highly innovative changes that help the customer take advantage of the environment. When you help the customer harness environmental forces, you truly become a strategic resource, resulting in higher revenues for your customer—and you.



## Action Summary

- Identify the key environmental forces influencing the current purchasing cycle.
- Develop a proposal that helps the customer succeed in the environment.
- Add maximum value by identifying opportunities to harness environmental forces and trends.

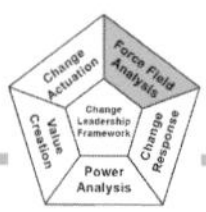


# SECRET # 17
# UNDERSTAND THE CLIENT'S LIFE SPACE

*Imagination was given to man to compensate him for what he is not, and a sense of humor was provided to console him for what he is.*

*—Robert Walpole*

## WHAT I NEED TO KNOW

German psychologist Kurt Lewin described life space as "the person and the psychological environment as it exists for him," including the person's experiences, learning, and goals. It is a multidimensional space, full of regions and forces. The different regions represent different mental, that is, psychological, situations or states. A change of location in the life space is a "behavior." The cause of the change from one location to another is what Lewin calls a "force." The drawing on the opposite page illustrates Lewin's life space concept, using a honeycomb as a metaphor. The honeycomb frame is the boundary of the person's life space. Each cell in the honeycomb is a psychological situation or state.

The core principle of change-centric selling is to help the client make changes in his life space—move from one of those cells to another.

The size of the life space depends on the person's development and experiences. A child would have a smaller life space than would an adult. For example, a toddler has difficulty feeding himself, whereas an adult can explore the realms of gourmet cooking. Therefore, Lewin suggested that people with bigger life spaces have more options. In other words, they have what I call a bigger "change space."

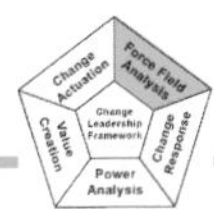


## What I Need to Do

Help the client make changes in her life space by understanding:

- The person's mental map of her life space
- The forces acting in the life space
- The set of available options, or the change space
- The desired changes

At the beginning of your relationship, your view of the customer's life space will be limited to a specific region or situation. So you will need to focus on the set of changes available to the person in that specific situation at that time; optimize locally. Over time, however, your view of the person's life space will expand and you will be able to assist the customer with higher-impact changes that optimize "globally" across the person's entire life space.

One of the biggest opportunities for change leaders is helping people expand their "change space" by removing perceived barriers to desired changes. Be sensitive to self-imposed barriers and add high value by helping the customer overcome them.



## Action Summary

- Understand how the customer views her situation.
- Identify change options.
- Help remove barriers to the desired situation.

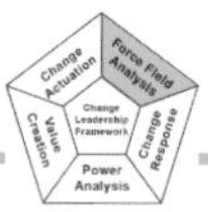


# SECRET # 18
# HARNESS THE FORCES

*There is one thing stronger than all the armies in the world, and that is an idea whose time has come.*

*—Victor Hugo*

## WHAT I NEED TO KNOW

You will be far more successful harnessing the forces of change than fighting them.

If after performing the force field analysis and understanding the client's life space, you determine that your product or service does not help the client make the desired change, you have three choices:

1. Disqualify the customer from your sales forecast and keep looking for prospective customers.
2. Change your product to fit the customer's needs by customizing your product, developing a new product, or acquiring the rights to sell a finished product.
3. Change the client's perception of his situation and the forces influencing it. The process of changing a customer's perception is what we typically think of as "selling." The difference is that the change leader is not selling a product or service, but rather is selling a different view of the forces influencing the client.

Whether you align your company to the customer's force field, or you change the customer's perception of it, you are harnessing the forces of change and guiding your company and the customer to a place that achieves the customer's desired result. When you have done that, you have become a true change leader.

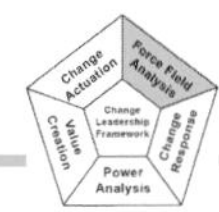




## What I Need to Do

Harness the forces of change by:

- Understanding the life space of the individual or organization
- Understanding the available changes, or "change space"
- Identifying the change that is most desirable and likely for the customer to achieve
- Identifying perceived barriers
- Aligning yourself with the Four Forces acting on the customer:
  - Needs
  - Behaviors
  - Strategies
  - Environment

Be mindful that the customer's perception is his reality. So, you will need both to work within the customer's reality and work to expand the customer's view of reality.



## Action Summary

- Align *with* forces, rather than *against* them, whenever possible.
- Wait, if necessary, until forces act to remove barriers.
- Be careful that perceptions are "accurate"—both the customer's and yours.

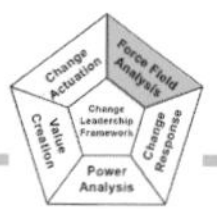


# SECRET # 19
# WHEREVER THERE IS CHANGE, THERE ARE FORCES

*All great results in our universe are founded in motions and forces the most minute.*

*—John Joly*

## WHAT I NEED TO KNOW

A principle of physics is that a body can only be in motion if a force has been applied to it. So by deduction, if the body is in motion, a force must have been applied.

This notion can lead you to powerful insights. Whenever you observe someone making a change, you should ask:

- What forces are driving this change?
  - Internal needs
  - Behavioral tendencies
  - Cognitive strategies
  - Environmental factors
- What situation is the person changing from?
- What situation is the person changing to?
- Where will the new situation lead? What will be the ultimate destination?

You may already naturally ask these questions. But it is likely that you don't give them much thought. The more mindfully and systematically you identify driving forces, the more effectively you will identify new revenue opportunities and the more effectively you will assist your customers in leading desired changes.

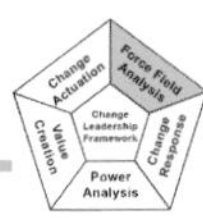




## What I Need to Do

Be aware of *all* the changes happening in your customer's organization.

Use the changes as vehicles to discover the forces at play in the organization. Start by asking questions like: What is driving this change? What is this change expected to achieve? As your customer provides answers, put them in the appropriate categories of the Four Forces model. Then, to complete your understanding, ask questions in the categories where you do not have answers.

As you develop a complete picture of the organization, add "color" to it by understanding which people are associated with the various forces. For example: Whose internal need is being satisfied by the change? Which people are aligned with the change and what power are they using to drive it?

Then, use your knowledge of the organization to align with power and identify opportunities.



## Action Summary

- Always have your "change detector" turned on to the highest sensitivity.
- See changes as opportunities to understand forces and characterize behavior.
- Align with changes and align with forces.

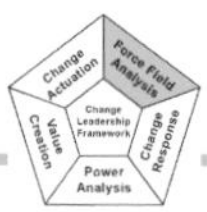


# SECRET # 20
# CHANGE REQUIRES CONSTANT FORCE

*Growth is never by chance; it is the result of forces working together.*

*—James Cash Penney*

## WHAT I NEED TO KNOW

Another principle of physics is that once in motion, a body will stay in motion unless an equal and opposite force is applied. I propose that this principle does not apply to human behavior—at least not in the realm of change leadership. How many times have you delegated a task, expecting it to be completed on schedule, as defined, only to discover later that it was not even close to being completed the way you expected? How many times have you gone on vacation and returned to find that little progress was made in your absence? It often seems that it is the energy of the salesperson that makes things happen.

As a generally applicable rule, I submit that humans are subject to an innate dampening effect, like a gravitational force, that tends to slow down motion over time. The dampening effect is similar to riding a bicycle up a hill. You continually have to add energy and keep pedaling in order to overcome the force of gravity. Otherwise, the bike eventually comes to a stop.

Change leaders must be cognizant of this "gravitational" force and be prepared to reinforce continually the change initiative. Remember, however, that you, yourself, are not a force. Your role is to keep the change initiative on track by maintaining the customer's awareness of the forces present in that situation.

## WHAT I NEED TO DO

The notion of gravitation forces raises a number of interesting questions for the salesperson.

- What factors in the customer's life space have a gravitational effect?
- Which of the Four Forces can be harnessed actively to add energy to the change?
  - Can internal needs and environmental forces be identified to counteract gravity?
  - Can the more passive forces of behavioral tendencies and cognitive strategies (e.g., habits or company processes) be harnessed to perpetuate the change?
- Can the salesperson, in the role of change leader, add energy to the change?



## ACTION SUMMARY

- Determine if forces are increasing or decreasing over time.
- Identify forces that tend to add energy to the change.
- Keep the heat on by maintaining the customer's awareness of the change forces.

# SECRET # 21 WHEREVER THERE IS A FORCE, THERE WILL BE CHANGE

*We must all obey the great law of change. It is the most powerful law of nature.*

*—Edmund Burke*

## WHAT I NEED TO KNOW

We previously said that wherever there is change, there are forces driving it. Of course, the inverse is also true. Wherever there is a force, there will be change—eventually.

Just keep in mind that change may not happen instantly. There may be forces that restrain the change from happening. As the driving and restraining forces increase, the only change may be increased tension. Eventually something will happen that either redirects the driving force or the restraining force, thereby releasing the tension and effecting the change. In the study of the psychology of change, we do not say the forces simply disappear. A change in a force must be associated with a change of behavior—whether an action or a change in someone's mind.

This principle can be used by the change leader to predict people's behavior. The more the change leader understands the person or organization's force field, the more accurately the change leader can predict the person's behaviors, the changes that will have highest likelihood of success, and the forces that can act as levers to stimulate change.

## What I Need to Do

Identify and map out the forces that are acting in the organization.

Classify the forces into "action" and "tension" categories, whereby the action category contains forces that are relatively uninhibited and, therefore, currently driving action; the tension category contains forces and sources of tension in the organization, where no action is currently happening.

Develop possible scenarios of where actions may lead and how tensions may be relieved.

Identify events that could trigger change.

Use this map of the force field to identify opportunities to help your customer and to develop a strategy for seizing them.



## Action Summary

- Identify forces.
- Predict resulting changes.
- Identify opportunities for adding value before, during, or after the changes.

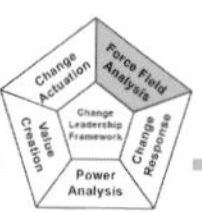

# SECRET # 22
# PEOPLE ARE ALWAYS IN MOTION

*Things do not change; we change.*
*—Henry David Thoreau*

## WHAT I NEED TO KNOW

An interesting, almost paradoxical concept is that people are always in motion. This contrasts the notion asserted by many psychologists that people's personalities are formed by the end of childhood and never fundamentally change afterward. Can you think of many examples of people in your business or life of whom you would say, "I would never trust that person," or "S/he will always be jerk," or "That person is truly kindhearted"?

Most of us would accept as true that in some ways people do not change. In fact, those dominant behavioral traits and tendencies are invaluable in helping predict people's responses. However, you should never assume a person or organization is static. People do not freeze into motionless statues. They are always in motion of some kind. They are always feeling forces of some kind. And they are always responding in some fashion. Therefore, people will certainly change, although some will change more than others. The question is not "Will the person change?" Rather, "How will the person change?"

In *Forceful Selling,* I stated the corollary to the third Law of Change as "People are always in motion, because they are always under the influence of forces." The key questions are then:

- Where is the person, right now, in her life space?
- What forces does she feel?
- What move will she make in her life space?
- When will she make the move?

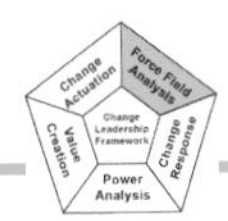



## What I Need to Do

The point of view that "people are always *changing*" speaks to the importance of perseverance and patience. The third Law of Change is "Wherever a force exists, it will tend to stimulate locomotion to a different space." So while the person may not be in a position to change, right now, if forces are present, you can be sure the person will eventually get off his chair and make a move.

Try to understand what forces are present. Then predict when the person may take action. Monitor the customer for signs of movement, ensuring you, rather than your competitor, are the salesperson present when the customer takes action.

Another point of view is that "people are always in *motion*." This begs the question, "Where is the person going?" Try to understand the answer and help the customer get there. Of course, as a change leader, do not accept trivial answers such as, "I am solving such-and-such problem." You are asking the question in the context of the person's life space. What internal need is the person pursuing?



## Action Summary

- Remember that behavioral tendencies are just one force among the Four Forces.
- Don't assume people won't change—the question is "When?" rather than "If?"
- Understand where the person is going.

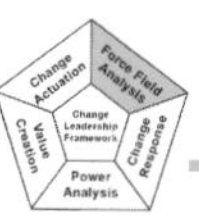


# SECRET # 23
# PEOPLE ARE SPRING-LOADED

*Man stores his emotions and desires like springs compressed, and then awaits the opportunity to release them.*

*—Brett Clay*

## WHAT I NEED TO KNOW

The principle that a body must be in motion if a force is applied assumes the body is rigid and that the force is completely transferred to the body. An interesting characteristic of human behavior is that people are not "rigid bodies" in the physics sense, but more like springs. When a force is applied to a spring, its energy is stored as "potential energy" before it is suddenly released and converted into motion.

People rarely immediately and continuously respond to every little stimulus, like a soccer ball bouncing around the soccer field in response to every kick. In fact, Lewin, Maslow, Jung, Freud, and every other psychologist would probably call that behavior neurotic. Rather, people store the forces they feel as potential energy and then they take action in finite amounts, called "discontinuous" motion. So people are tricky to understand because they are composed of many springs of different sizes. It can be a challenge to discover the size of these "springs" and what will trigger their release.

While in some cases change happens slowly and incrementally, the process of change leadership is often similar to firing a catapult. Much energy is required to load the payload and compress the spring. Then, a trigger is pulled and the change happens suddenly.

## What I Need to Do

As a change leader, seek to understand:

- What forces are stored in the organization?
- In which people are the forces stored?
- How powerful are the forces? How much energy is stored?
- What will trigger the release of the energy into action?

Once you understand where the springs are, map your strategy for which ones to avoid ("land mines"), which ones to trigger, and in what order to trigger them. Be careful not to trigger springs prematurely as it is often more effective to line people up for one big push in unison. Think of pulling a bandage off with one, quick motion. The change will be finished before people realize and the perceived pain will be much smaller.

Remember, most of the effort goes into loading and lining up the various springs for action. Once the triggering event happens, change may happen quickly. Be sure to set expectations accordingly among your change coalition.



## Action Summary

- Be prepared for people to act suddenly.
- Identify sensitive issues and people who could spring in your face ("land mines").
- Try to have the springs release at the same time.

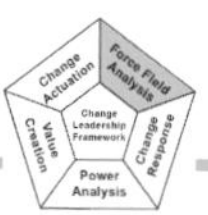


# SECRET # 24
# CUSTOMER SATISFACTION IS IMPOSSIBLE

*Poor is not the person who has little, but the person who craves more.*

*—Lucius Annaeus Seneca*

## WHAT I NEED TO KNOW

The underlying principle of Maslow's Hierarchy of Needs is that as soon as a person has satisfied a need at one level in the hierarchy, the person will immediately feel a need at the next level. This leads to the conclusion that people can never be satisfied, which presents both opportunities and challenges to the change leader.

Every salesperson would like to have "poor" customers who crave more and more, rather than become satisfied with very little. The opportunity is to deliver more when the customer inevitably wants more.

The first challenge is to manage carefully the customer's present expectations, resulting in a happy customer. A principle of quality management is that quality means meeting expectations. So, ensure that your customer is happy with the results of the current change initiative by carefully setting expectations and then exceeding them.

The other important challenge for the salesperson is to evolve with the customer's evolving needs. Once you deliver a change to satisfy one need, the customer immediately has another "need" beyond that. There is nothing irrational or wrong with the customer wanting more; it's called progress. But to stay in the game and continue to satisfy growing needs, you will have to grow, as well.

## What I Need to Do

Identify the person's or organization's "hierarchy of needs." Forecast what the person will need after the first need has been satisfied. Then forecast what will be needed after the second, and so on.

Develop your capability to satisfy the customer's evolving needs. Be creative. In today's world of virtual teams, virtual work forces, and virtual companies, you may be able to partner jointly with other companies or subcontract part of the delivery. In fact, the more "strategic" a change leader you become, the more you will need to subcontract the implementation of the change.

Whether you personally deliver the product or service, rely on team members in your company, or rely on subcontractors at other companies, you must carefully manage the customer's expectations and ensure your delivery exceeds those expectations. Delivery is job # 1. Deliver outstanding results.

One of the most important change leadership skills, therefore, is systematic project management. Continually build these skills.

## Action Summary

- Identify the customer's hierarchy of needs.
- Develop your ability to deliver.
- Be fanatic about project management and delivery.

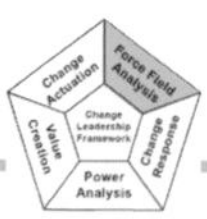

# Secret # 25 Observation Is Different From Reality

*Seek simplicity and distrust it.*

*—Alfred North Whitehead*

## What I Need to Know

Another complication of humans is that what you see on the outside is not what is on the inside. Most of the time, when we observe someone's "behavior," that is, the changes the person makes, we may only be able to observe the force that triggered the release of the spring. It would be incorrect to assume that is the only force driving the person's behavior. Many forces drive the person's actions, the summation of which is called the "resultant" force that points in a specific direction from one space to another (within the person's life space).

The resultant force is a "theoretical" force because it does not actually exist—only the individual forces actually exist. The resultant force is the easiest to observe primarily because we can observe the actual movement from one space to another and we can develop some assumptions about the force that must have caused the movement. It is much more difficult to decompose the resultant force into the "real" forces to be observed and measured individually.

The key point is to be careful in making observations and conclusions about people. As a salesperson, you have found that driving simplicity usually helps people make decisions and take action. You will be most effective driving agreement for change, however, if you understand people's different perspectives and the forces under the surface.

## What I Need to Do

Be careful not to make erroneous assumptions and be ever vigilant in looking for the actual forces. The process of decomposing the forces is similar to the cliché of peeling an onion. For every force you think you understand, ask the question, "What forces are driving this one?"

When someone, especially if that someone is you, says, "It's simple," remember that simple minds see things simply. It is true that all things are ultimately simple. But don't fool yourself into believing you have a complete understanding. Always ask yourself, "What is under the surface that I am not seeing?"

Be an effective change leader by getting under the surface to address underlying issues and find additional ways to achieve agreement.



## Action Summary

- Remember, what you see on the outside may not be what is on the inside.
- Dig under the surface to discover what is on the inside.
- Drive agreement and change by looking under the surface to address concerns and find agreeable terms.

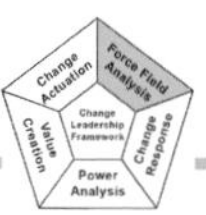


# Secret # 26
# The Four Forces Are Always Present

*Is it ever happiness that we seek? No, it is the free play of those forces that happen to be the most recent ones in us.*

*—Andre Gide (at age 80)*

## What I Need to Know

Another way to state this secret is that any change is caused by a combination of all Four Forces. I pointed out earlier that a person cannot be separated from her environment. Similarly, a person cannot be separated from herself or her own internal needs, behavioral tendencies, and cognitive strategies. Therefore, any change that is made (remember that Lewin uses "change" and "behavior" synonymously) must be in the context of all Four Forces.

Why worry about all the Four Forces, if the person just cares about a particular force? Let's say the organization wants to respond to a new regulatory requirement in the environment. Seems simple enough. But, the organization's goals, systems, and culture all play a role in how the organization responds to this environmental force. In fact, the environment also plays a role, because the organization could choose to change the environment and conduct business in a different regulatory jurisdiction.

Earlier when I talked about observation being different from reality, I discussed the concept of the resultant force—a single force that represents the sum of all forces. The same concept applies here. Think of all forces as having four dimensions.

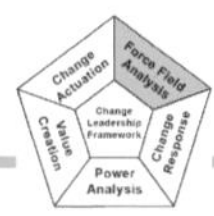




## What I Need to Do

Whenever you observe a particular force, make sure you understand it in the context of all four dimensions:

- Internal needs
- Behavioral tendencies
- Cognitive strategies
- Environmental factors

When you observe a particular change, ask, "How are the Four Forces driving this change?"

Now that you have your "force detector" turned on and the antenna up, make a habit of looking for all four dimensions. At least once a day, perform the exercise of picking someone, whether it is someone in your customer base, or a random person in a public space, and try to imagine the Four Forces that person feels in that moment. Then, strike up a conversation and see if you can validate your guesses—you may find you were completely wrong! Remember, what you see on the outside may not be what is inside.

## Action Summary

- Understand specific changes and forces in the context of all four dimensions.
- Always validate your understanding with the customer.
- Remember, people's perception of the forces around them changes constantly.

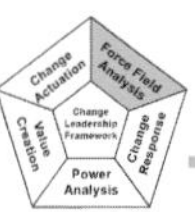


# Secret # 27
# Stronger the Force, Stronger the Movement

*Only people who feel compelled by great forces achieve great things.*

*—Brett Clay*

## What I Need to Know

A basic principle of physics is that the larger the force applied to a body of a given mass, the faster it will accelerate. Similarly, the stronger a person experiences a force, the quicker the person will respond to it and the faster the person will make the change.

The key word is "experiences." People generally experience forces in the following phases or levels:

1. **Awareness.** A person must be aware and "mindful" that the force exists. If a person's mind is occupied with something else, the person may not even become aware of the force.
2. **Appraisal.** The person appraises the force's size and urgency and makes an initial judgment about the appropriate response. Does it merit an immediate "fight-or-flight" response, or at the other end of the spectrum, does it merit no response?
3. **Intellectualized**. The person develops an "intellectual," unemotional understanding of the force. For example, when you read about a natural disaster that destroys people's homes, you are intellectualizing the event.
4. **Internalized**. The person feels the force at a deep emotional and cognitive level. It is the "a-ha" moment. It is the full appreciation that can only be gained by actually surviving the natural disaster and seeing your own house destroyed.

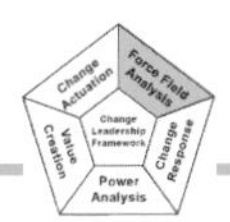




## What I Need to Do

First, determine at what level the customer is experiencing the force. Then, try to guide the customer through awareness, appraisal, and intellectualizing by asking questions. For example, "What do you think about that?" "How is that affecting you?"

Assess the person's level of internalization by asking, "How do you *feel* about that?" You have limited influence over internalization, so you may have to wait patiently. For example, how can you get someone fully to internalize, say, the importance of auto insurance until they have been involved in an accident? In some cases, you may even want to use internalization as a way to qualify prospects.

Of course, as a change leader, you want the customer to experience the force as strongly as possible. Be creative, but ethical, in identifying ways to raise the customer's awareness, help the customer perform an accurate appraisal, develop a complete understanding, and fully appreciate the magnitude of the force.



## Action Summary

- Identify at what level the force is being experienced.
- Determine the perceived strength of the force.
- Reinforce the force.

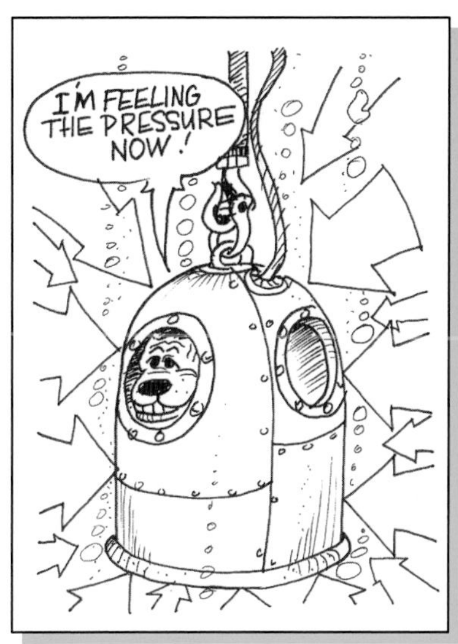

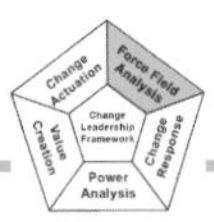

# SECRET # 28
# EVERY FORCE HAS EQUAL RESISTANCE

*People are more like walls than windows; they're hard to see into and the harder you push, the harder they push back.*

*—Brett Clay*

## WHAT I NEED TO KNOW

One of Isaac Newton's basic principles of physics is the concept of equal and opposite forces. When you are sitting in a chair, right now, you are exerting a downward force on it, which is your mass times the acceleration of gravity. The chair is pushing upward on you with equal force. This concept from physics has interesting implications for the change leader studying a person's force field.

Does it mean that for every one of a person's needs, say, safety for example, that there is an equal force pushing back on that need? That is correct. Lewin's second law states that a force will result in a movement. So, if a force exists (remember that according to Maslow the force can only exist if the need has not been satisfied), but there is no movement, then there must be an equal force pushing back, resisting the movement.

This introduces another important concept described by Lewin: tension. Lewin says these driving forces and equal resisting forces are in tension, which he defines as the sum of the driving and resisting forces associated with a specific change. For example, the tension in the seat of the chair you are sitting on is twice your weight.

As a change leader, one of your most important tasks is to identify the resisting forces that are keeping the person or situation in tension. Each of those forces will have to be removed or overcome to reduce tension and execute change.

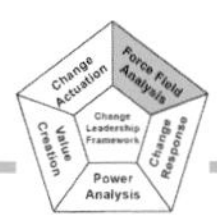




## What I Need to Do

For every force you have mapped in the client's life space, identify an equal force that is opposing it and is restraining change from occurring.

Sometimes restraining forces may be subtle or hidden. If you cannot find an equal and opposite force, then you have to ask, "Why hasn't this change occurred already? Why does this force exist? Why hasn't it been satisfied?" The answers will uncover the resisting forces.

Think of several ways each resisting force could be reduced or eliminated.

Resisting forces often take the form of major obstacles, especially when they involve habitual behavior like smoking or eating. In those cases, it may seem easier to increase the driving forces rather than reduce the resisting forces. That may be true. But reducing resistance is always more effective. Less resistance requires less force to overcome it, requiring less effort to make the change and less effort to maintain the change (e.g., weight loss).



## Action Summary

- Identify at least one force that opposes each driving force.
- Brainstorm ways to reduce or eliminate restraining forces.
- Develop a plan to reduce resistance and validate it with the customer.

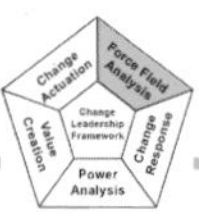


# Secret # 29
# Forces and Changes Are Like Fans

*Does the flap of a butterfly's wings in Brazil set off a tornado in Texas?*

*—Edward Lorenz*

## What I Need to Know

I previously mentioned that every force has an equal and opposite force. But it doesn't stop there. Every force also induces a cascade of other forces. Remember how the chair you are sitting on is pushing up against the weight of your body? If the chair is pushing up, according to Newton, it must also be pushing down. And indeed it is. The chair is pushing down into the floor with the force of your mass, plus its mass times the acceleration of gravity.

But you say, "If the chair is pushing down into the floor, then the floor must be pushing up on the chair." And indeed it is. You can see how the forces continue to cascade—until something far away may feel the original force. The cascading effect is similar to how the force of an earthquake in one part of the ocean can cause a wave that arrives on the other side of the world in a matter of hours.

Because forces and changes are like opposite sides of the same coin, changes have the same effect. One change causes another change.

Not only do forces and changes induce a cascade of other forces and changes in one direction, but they spread out like a fan in multiple directions, effectively multiplying. Keep in mind that the resisting forces will multiply accordingly.

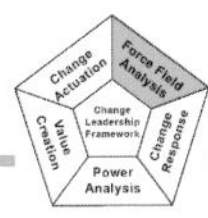




## WHAT I NEED TO DO

Assess and map the fan out by following these four steps.

First, indentify what other forces are being induced by each previously identified force. How will they fan out? Who is being impacted and how?

Second, forecast what other changes will be induced by a particular change. Again ask, "Who will be impacted and how?"

Third, for each of the analyses above, identify a change for each force and a force for each change.

Finally, identify at least one resisting force for each force. Try to put names of people and organizations on all forces and changes.

How exhaustively you perform this analysis should depend on the size of the order at stake and the complexity of the proposed change initiative. For example, if you are an information technology system integrator proposing to change a business process that will impact tens of thousands of people in a Fortune 100 company, you will likely be expected to perform an exhaustive analysis.

## ACTION SUMMARY

- Identify how forces are fanning out in the organization.
- Forecast how changes might cascade through the organization.
- Identify forces that will resist the changes.

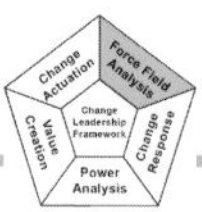


# Secret # 30
# People Make Poor Computers

*I am indeed amazed when I consider how weak my mind is and how prone to error.*

*—Rene Descartes*

## What I Need to Know

After performing a discovery of the person's life and change spaces, you would have a keen understanding of your customer and a model of all the forces influencing the organization. That could be a bit bewildering. But that is exactly what the customer is facing—a bewildering array of forces and options.

As I mentioned previously, all of those forces will ultimately add and subtract until there is essentially one force, the "resultant force" that represents the total.

$$Resultant\ Force = \{driving\ forces\} + \{resisting\ forces\}$$

Similarly, all the changes would result in one net change, called the "resultant change." For example, if you take two steps to the right, one step forward, one step to the left, and one step backward, then the net change is one step to the right.

$$Resultant\ Change = \sum Changes$$

The people in the organization are like computers, constantly calculating and recalculating these equations determining the net forces they feel and the responses they will make.

But alas, people are not computers. Many business scholars have written about how poorly human beings make these calculations. In an effort to simplify the computations, people make many false judgments, assumptions, and conclusions.

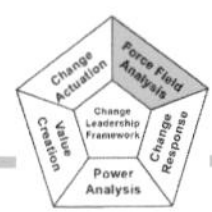




## What I Need to Do

Use your understanding of the customer's life and change spaces to predict what changes he may want to make.

Because people's computational capacity is not perfect, their calculations will generate different results, even if they use the same input. Therefore, develop various scenarios for how they may view their life space and change space.

Of course, it would be far easier simply to ask the customer for his views—and you should. But getting a customer to disclose parts of his personality that he himself may not fully understand can be difficult. Also, in order to fully understand and predict your customer's behaviors, you have to try to put yourself in his mind, anyway.

Last, never assume you can predict behavior with 100 percent accuracy. People will surprise you when you least expect it. So, always have contingencies.



## Action Summary

- Remember that most people find it difficult to "compute" the forces in their lives.
- Add value by helping the customer sort through the forces.
- Use your understanding to predict behavior and desired changes.

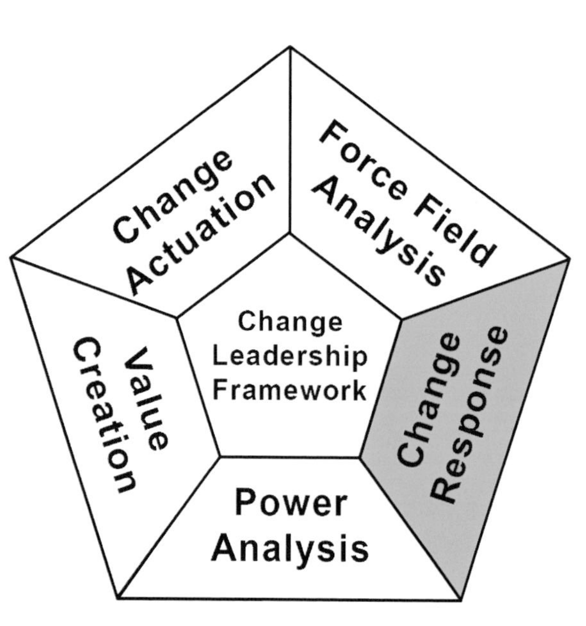
Change Actuation
Force Field Analysis
Change Leadership Framework
Value Creation
Change Response
Power Analysis

# CHANGE RESPONSE ANALYSIS

## THE SECOND DISCIPLINE

# INTRODUCTION

# TO

# CHANGE RESPONSE ANALYSIS

## What is it?

Change response analysis is the process of understanding how a customer responds to the forces she or he feels.

How many times have you thought you could predict someone's behavior, only to be completely surprised? The underlying premise of change response analysis is that no two people respond identically to identical forces. For example, two people can be served the same food from the same pan and they will respond very differently to it (at least they do around my house!). Therefore, understanding a person's force field is a necessary, but not sufficient, requirement for predicting that person's behavior.

This section also includes descriptions of common cognitive biases that influence people's change responses. Effective change leaders recognize the influence of these biases and guide the customer to objective decisions.

## Why is it important?

Every action people take is a response to some force he or she feels. Understanding how people respond is critical for helping them take appropriate action—and for you to win the sale.

## How is it new or different?

Traditional solution-centric selling focuses on understanding the impacts of problems and the benefits of solving them. That approach positions the salesperson simply as a purveyor of benefits—like a vendor selling hotdogs from a cart. The belief is that the louder the vendor shouts the benefits, the more likely the customer will be to take action.

Simply identifying the benefits of making a change is not sufficient to spur action. Change-centric selling addresses the underlying psychology of making a change. By operating as a counselor and leading the customer through the process of recognition and change, rather than operating as a solution-and-benefits consultant, the change-centric salesperson succeeds more often and creates far more value.

### What are the common misconceptions?

Marketers and sales managers tend to view solution-centric selling as the pinnacle of selling, using the term to refer to any effort by a salesperson to understand the customer's problem and to uncover the benefits of solving it—in other words, building a value proposition. Certainly stopping long enough to develop a purchase justification will be more successful than simply quoting price and delivery terms and waiting by the fax machine to receive an order. But, sales managers who believe the solution-centric approach will remain competitive are going to get blindsided by the Internet and global competitors. The Internet now gives customers the power to develop their own solutions and justifications. Only by operating as counselors and leading clients through the change process will salespeople be able to create profitable differentiation.

### What are the key take-aways & how do I put them in action?

Understand how customers respond to the forces they feel and how they make changes. Don't start on the purchase justification—in fact, don't even start defining a solution—until you understand how the organization is responding. Then, assist the customer in making the appropriate changes to achieve his goals. Your customers will be pleased and your sales will soar.

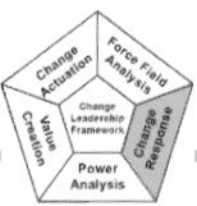


# SECRET # 31
# CHANGE YOUR PARADIGM

*Innovation and change supersede all problems and solutions.*
*—Brett Clay*

## WHAT I NEED TO KNOW

In Section 2, we discussed how a problem is just the tip of the iceberg, a superficial symptom of everything going on under the surface, a mere brick in the road on the way to a person's goals. Change-centric selling is about shifting the salesperson's paradigm from asking the customer, "What is your problem?" to "What are you changing?"

Of course, the questions are disguised differently. For example, you might ask the customer, "Tell me about your competitors" or "What are the key issues driving your business, these days?" But the key question the change leader seeks to understand is "How is the customer responding?"

Once the change leader understands how the customer is responding to the forces and associated changes, the change leader can align with those forces and harness them to assist the customer in achieving the change.

Once you understand change-centric selling and change leadership, it becomes apparent that this really is a profound paradigm shift. The question, "What are you changing?" is much more proactive, constructive, and progressive than, "What problem are you fixing?" You are not just helping the customer prevent an imminent failure. You are helping the customer move forward and achieve new accomplishments.

## What I Need to Do

Change your paradigm from asking, "What is the problem?" or "What do you need?" to "What are you changing?"

Follow through by asking:

- Why?
- How?

Then get at the fundamental issues:

- What forces are driving this change? (This is a more palatable way to ask, "What forces are you experiencing?")
- How are you responding (to those forces)?

Your key task from that point will be understanding how the customer responds to change and assisting the customer in achieving it.

## Action Summary

- Ask: What are you changing?
- Discover: What is driving the change?
- Observe: How does the customer respond?

Vs.

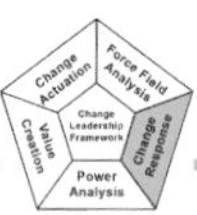

# SECRET # 32
# UNDERSTAND THE JACK IN THE BOX

*Horse sense is what keeps horses from betting on what people will do.*

*—Raymond Nash*

## WHAT I NEED TO KNOW

I don't know about you, but people seem to have so many different ways of thinking that I have completely given up the practice of assuming. I no longer "assume" anything about anyone. Once I see someone do something once, I know they are capable of doing it again. If I see them do it twice, then I know they are likely to do it again in the future. However, if the circumstances are slightly different in the future, then they might do something else in the future.

The process of characterizing how a person behaves under various conditions is similar to the scientific notion of characterizing a "black box." The idea of a black box is that it is completely opaque and therefore, you have no ability to see inside. The only way to determine its contents is to make inferences based on how it responds to various stimuli.

People are black boxes, also. It is impossible to see inside people's minds and souls. As a change leader, you can only observe how people respond under various conditions.

When a new force or change confronts a person, you would like to have an idea of how that person will respond. Is the black box suddenly going to pop open in your face, like a jack-in-the-box, with a strong response? Who is the "Jack" in the box?

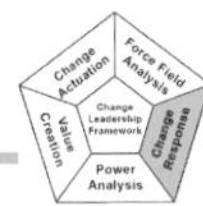



## What I Need to Do

Determine the characteristics of the "Jack" in the box.

Be sure to characterize people by their behaviors and actions, rather than their words.

Be aware of the common biases that could cloud your observations and lead to inaccurate characterizations.

Remember that people's behavior is situational. Next time, they may not react the same way because something might be slightly different. So, take careful note of all the variables in the situation.

Every interaction is an opportunity to characterize the person. Be cognizant of the situation and how the person responded.

Before each interaction, form a hypothesis about how the person will react and test your hypothesis. Sometimes you may be able to plainly ask, "If [some event] were to happen, what would you do?"



## Action Summary

- Measure people by their actions, not their words.
- Note how situations are similar and different.
- People may never behave the way you predict, so always be prepared for a surprise when the jack-in-the-box opens.

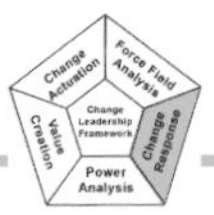


# SECRET # 33
# UNDERSTAND COPING STRATEGIES

*Problems are not the problem; coping is the problem.*
*—Virginia Satir*

## WHAT I NEED TO KNOW

In order to characterize a person's change response, we first need to understand general principles of how people process stimuli, called "coping" strategies. Wayne Weiten and Margaret Lloyd suggested three generic strategies:

1. **Appraisal**. People typically first appraise the force, or situation, and make judgments whether to (a) deny its existence, (b) delay dealing with it, (c) devalue its importance, or (d) dig in and do something about it.

2. **Emoting**. After appraising, people typically experience emotions. Eventually, people have to construct a solution to yield an improvement in the situation. In the meantime, they may become distracted or attempt to demolish the force, which makes the situation worse. People's emotions can either reinforce the construction of solutions or reinforce distractive and destructive behaviors.

3. **Problem solving**. Finally, once people have emoted constructively and opted for action, they problem solve by (a) defining the problem, (b) researching solutions, (c) choosing a course of action, (d) taking action.

## What I Need to Do

As you characterize your customer's change response, first note how the customer appraises the situation. Of course, you hope the customer will dig in and take immediate action. But if the person goes into denial, devalues the importance, or otherwise delays action, you will have to watch patiently and, if possible, gently guide the person until he acknowledges the necessity of action.

Keep your expectations low for your ability to influence the person's appraisal. Most people feel their appraisals are very personal and may even resent what they would consider an intrusion into their personal identities.

Next, note if the person emotes constructively or destructively. If the person is committed to action, you need to spring into action and quickly bring value to the problem-solving process. If the person is distracted with destructive emotions, especially a sense of helplessness, you may want to offer assistance and support to guide the person into the problem-solving mode. But you'll want to assess carefully how much of your investment is appropriate.



## Action Summary

- Observe how the customer appraises, emotes, and problem solves in response to specific situations.
- Move quickly when the customer is disposed to take action.
- Patiently wait, or possibly disengage, if the customer's response is not constructive.

# SECRET # 34
# STAY AWAY FROM CHICKENS

*It was character that got us out of bed, commitment that moved us into action, and discipline that enabled us to follow through.*

*—Zig Ziglar*

## WHAT I NEED TO KNOW

The Six Change Types model I described in *Forceful Selling* describes six common ways that people adapt to the forces they experience. The first change-type is the "Chicken."

The Chicken is one of the two neurotic change types. This person is not able to adapt successfully to any situation and simply keeps changing. This person appears to go randomly from change to change, oblivious to any risk, and he does not make significant progress on any change attempted. The Chicken has a short attention span, a high level of anxiety, and is emotionally unstable. Since the person often changes before having an opportunity to learn and become proficient, his confidence is damaged and his driving need is esteem. Because this person always makes changes, it may appear that he is open to making adjustments in notions and activities. However, the person is actually reluctant to commit himself and never completely follows through. Therefore, his openness is only superficial. The figure below shows the Chicken's profile.

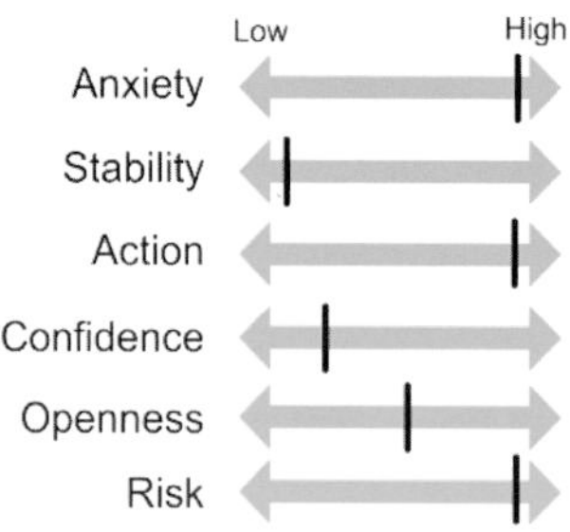

## What I Need to Do

As a salesperson and change leader, your resources will be depleted before you are able to help the Chicken complete a change. Therefore, you should quickly disengage from customers who display the characteristics of the Chicken profile.

Can you think of people in your business or life who have one or more of those characteristics? Are they easy to deal with? Or do you try to avoid them?

Perform an ongoing return on investment (ROI) calculation to determine whether further investment will be profitable. If not, stop your losses and move on.



## Action Summary

- Use the Six Change Types model to characterize people's change response.
- Disengage from Chickens.
- Continuously calculate your ROI and know your investment stop loss.

# SECRET # 35
# FOLLOW THE CHAMELEONS

*Enjoying success requires the ability to adapt. Only by being open to change will you have a true opportunity to get the most from your talent.*

*—Nolan Ryan*

## WHAT I NEED TO KNOW

The second change-type is the "Chameleon."

The Chameleon is an "early adopter" of changes. She has high confidence and is comfortable being alone ahead of the herd. She does not have strong anxieties, but instead is naturally comfortable with change. She enjoys exploration and discovery, and for her, change seems to come quickly and effortlessly. She has a high level of energy and is action oriented. She has low tolerance for inactive people who are slow to make changes. She has a high tolerance for risk, but, unlike the Chicken, her risks are calculated and controlled. Because of her high confidence and action-oriented nature, if a change results in failure, it barely slows her down; it is just a bump in the road. The Chameleon has the highest level of openness of all of the change types. Chameleons are true change leaders. But because few people are so adept at change, their numbers are few. The figure below shows the Chameleon's profile.

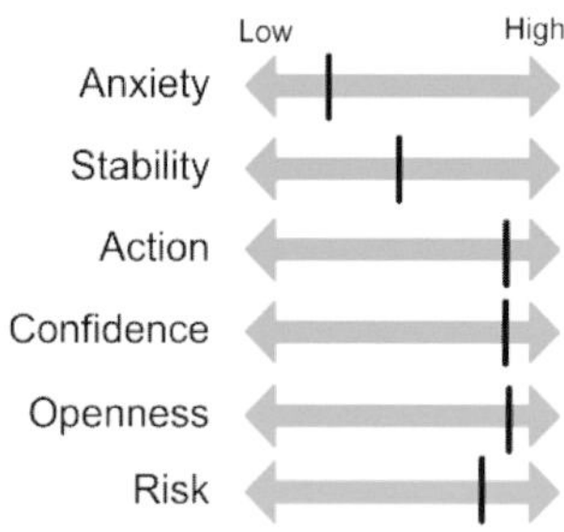

## What I Need to Do

If you find a Chameleon, follow her—she has already found the best path! You may want to solicit this person to be a mentor or coach.

Listen intently and move quickly when assisting Chameleons with change—they do not have patience for slow processes.

Stress the novelty and innovation in the change you are suggesting. Also, focus on the vision for the future, as Chameleons are not interested in the past or in paths that have already been tried.

View your Chameleon customers as harbingers of future trends. They may not be tremendously profitable because they comprise a market of one. But if you apply what you learn from Chameleons to other customers, you may open up whole new, highly profitable opportunities.

Can you think of someone in your business or personal life who most resembles the Chameleon characteristics? See what you can learn from that person.



## Action Summary

- Use Chameleons as indicators of possible future trends.
- Emphasize and deliver innovation.
- Learn from Chameleons and identify new opportunities.

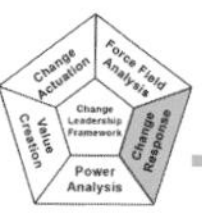


# SECRET # 36
# HELP THE GEESE

*We have to adapt and overcome, that's all we can do.*
*—Frank Knight*

## WHAT I NEED TO KNOW

The third change-type is the "Canadian Geese."

For the Geese, change has always been part of their lives. In fact, their lives in the flock depend on change. They understand they will perish if the flock does not move south for the winter. They are adept at change—regularly making measured, wholesale, strategic changes—moving the flock across the world for better opportunities. However, because of the size of the organization (the flock), Geese must strategically plan for change. Their anxiety is relatively low, but not the lowest, because they live under a constant cloud of environmental forces. Geese are also emotionally stable and cope with environmental forces confidently and strategically. Because of the magnitude of changes they undertake and the size of their organization that must implement the changes, they arguably have the most action. Geese may appear to be very open to change, and while this is generally true, the changes they make and the risks they take are calculated, planned, and tested. The figure below shows the Geese's profile.

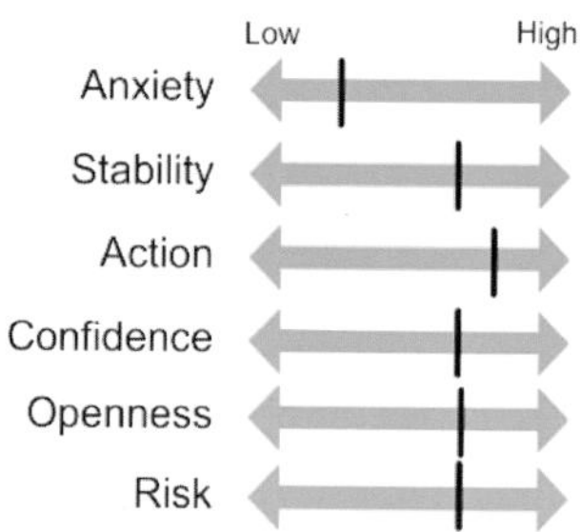

## What I Need to Do

Geese may present your biggest revenue opportunities and may be your "best" customers. However, they may require the most resources and preparation.

Engage with Geese in a methodical, highly professional manner.

Remember that Geese require significant planning and validation before they take actions that affect the entire organization. Eighty percent of their efforts may be used in planning, with execution consuming just 20 percent. Try to structure your engagement such that you are not providing free consulting during the planning. Remember, Geese consider planning to be 80 percent of the value.

Recognize that people may temporarily behave like Geese when implementing large-scale changes in their businesses or their lives. Add value by helping them with their planning. This will lower the anxieties that naturally accompany big changes.



## Action Summary

- Develop a strong set of planning tools and techniques that can assist your customers.
- Be prepared for a long sales process and try to get paid along the way.
- Actively engage Geese, as they may form the core of your business.

# SECRET # 37
# COUNT ON THE BEAVERS

*Patience, persistence and perspiration make an unbeatable combination for success.*

*—Napoleon Hill*

## WHAT I NEED TO KNOW

The fourth change-type is the "Beaver."

The Beaver is the most stable of all of the change types. The Beaver stays close to home (i.e., the current situation) and makes small incremental changes. He perceives that large-scale change brings large-scale risk, which he does not see as necessary. Over time, his constant, incremental changes may have a large impact. For example, the Beaver's lodge becomes very large, dams the stream and forms a lake many times wider than the original stream. The Beaver is full of action and activity and is extremely confident in his ability to make the changes he has defined. However, he is not quite confident enough to explore entirely new territories, and he will abandon his current situation only as a last resort. The Beaver's tolerance for risk is relatively well adjusted. He does not seek risk, nor does he fear it. The figure below shows the Beaver's profile.

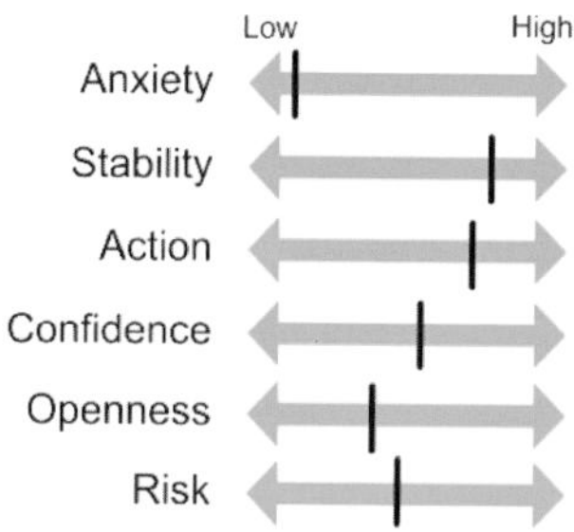

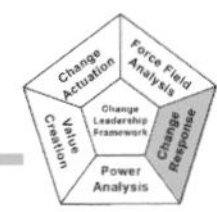



## WHAT I NEED TO DO

Beavers can be highly profitable, long-time, repeat customers. So you will want to cultivate and maintain your relationship.

Beavers are extremely busy, so you will need to be persistent in getting their attention.

Be careful to propose changes that fall within the boundaries of the Beaver's current vision. Only propose significant changes if a response to a specific environmental force is warranted.

Beavers do have a long-term vision, which they approach systematically over time. The more you can help the Beaver with that long-term vision and participate in it, the more profitable a customer he will be for you.

Whenever possible, try to engage in long-term contracts with Beavers. However, make sure you don't lock yourself into static businesses that prevent you from evolving with the broader market.



## ACTION SUMMARY

- Develop Beavers as long-time customers.
- Keep proposals within the Beaver's current vision.
- Be careful to evolve faster than your customer and don't get locked into status quo.

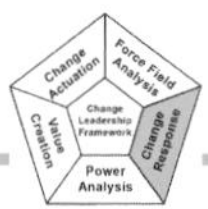


# SECRET # 38
# COMFORT THE MULES

*Adapt or perish, now as ever, is nature's inexorable imperative.*

*—H. G. Wells*

## WHAT I NEED TO KNOW

The fifth change-type is the "Mule."

The Mule is reluctant to change. The Mule may have slightly more anxieties than the Chameleon, but like the Chameleon, the Mule is not driven by anxiety. Unlike the Chameleon, however, the Mule is naturally uncomfortable with change. She values consistency, familiarity, and safety and has relatively low openness. She does not necessarily lack self-esteem, but she does lack the courage to be bold in exploring the unknown. To the Mule, the unknown seems mysterious so she prefers to rely on others to report their findings. Although the Mule could exhibit a high level of activity, those activities are tightly constrained, and she is not considered action-oriented compared to the Chameleon, Geese, and Beaver. The Mule has a low tolerance for risk, and if she perceives a change as a threat to her safety, the Mule may vehemently resist that change. The figure below shows the Mule's profile.

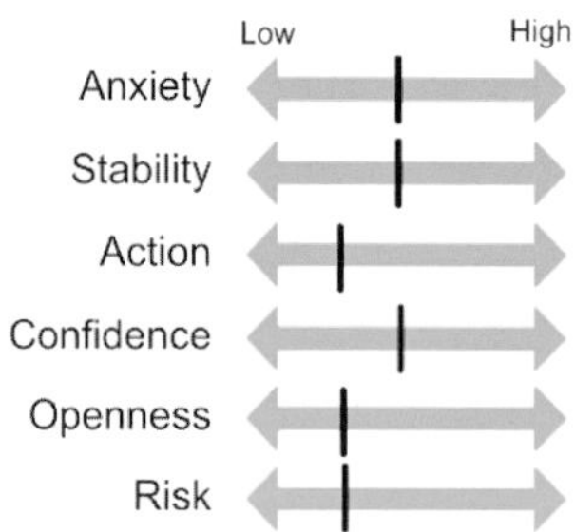

## What I Need to Do

While Mules are reluctant to change, they do not refuse to change. Their change response is limited to only the strongest forces. They cope with weaker forces through denial or devaluation. This leaves you with two choices:

1. Suggest only the smallest of changes to Mules.
2. Suggest changes that respond to only the most powerful of forces.

Your success in selling a change that falls between those two extremes will be limited at best. Therefore, your first task is to qualify the Mule and disengage if the Mule perceives your product or service to be in the middle.

Your chief task is to help the Mule feel comfortable with the change process. Do this by increasing her familiarity as much as possible, using demonstrations, references, white papers, videos, and so on. Also, reinforce the dissatisfactions of the status quo and the benefits of the change, being as visual as possible.



## Action Summary

- Engage Mules only with very small changes or changes that address their most powerful perceived forces.
- Disengage if you are perceived as addressing a medium-sized force.
- Focus on increasing the Mule's comfort level.

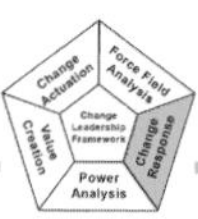


# SECRET # 39
# STAY AWAY FROM TURTLES

*It often takes more courage to change one's opinion than to stick to it.*
*—George Christoph Lichtenberg*

## WHAT I NEED TO KNOW

The sixth change type is the "Turtle."

The Turtle is the other neurotic change type. The Turtle is plagued by anxieties, perhaps second only to those of the Chicken. Whereas the Chicken copes with anxieties by occupying himself with activities, the Turtle's coping mechanism is to withdraw into his shell, close himself off from the reality of the world, and form his own reality inside his shell. He is close-minded, fiercely resists change, and refuses to acknowledge the changes occurring all around him. Because of the strong effect of his coping mechanisms, the Turtle may appear to be slightly more stable than the Chicken. But the Turtle lacks the confidence to acknowledge reality—let alone venture into the unknown. The Turtle also has the lowest action-orientation, risk tolerance, confidence, and openness of all the change types. The figure below shows the Turtle's profile.

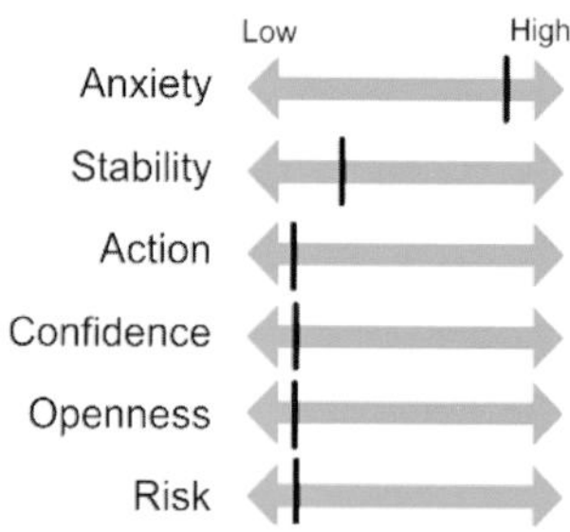

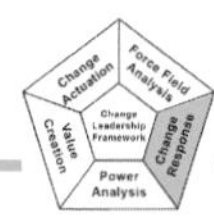




## WHAT I NEED TO DO

Your resources will be depleted before you succeed in helping a Turtle make changes. As the saying goes, "You can lead a horse to water, but you can't make him drink."

It is truly a sad and frustrating experience to watch a Turtle withdraw into his shell and forfeit seemingly beautiful opportunities.

However, you have responsibilities to your company, yourself, and your family. Those responsibilities do not permit you to expend resources that generate zero return. In fact, you could experience a negative return if the Turtle snaps at you when he perceives you are "attacking" his status quo. Only the Turtle must take responsibility for his change response.

Therefore, do everyone a favor and disengage from the Turtle as quickly as possible.



## ACTION SUMMARY

- Quickly identify and disengage from Turtles.
- Do not attempt to engage the Turtle if he snaps in defense of his status quo.
- Gradually wean yourself of any existing customers who prevent you from evolving your business.

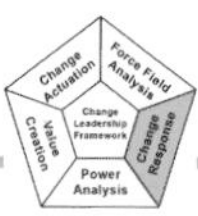


# SECRET # 40
# DO A REALITY CHECK

*Reality is nothing more than a collective hunch.*
*—Lily Tomlin*

## WHAT I NEED TO KNOW

When characterizing a person's change response, the change leader must be aware of differing views of reality. When Lewin described his concepts of forces and life space, he stipulated that they are dependent on people's perceptions, which he called "cognitive structure."

When I introduced the concept of change response analysis, I mentioned that people respond very differently to the same forces. There are many reasons why people respond differently. They may have different needs, levels of extroversion, openness, or risk tolerance—the list goes on.

But another reason merits further discussion. People may respond differently to the same forces because they actually do not see the same forces. One person sees one force, another person sees another force, and a third person sees the forces as identical. For example, the figure on the opposite page shows a train in motion. Is the train coming or going? Or is it even in motion? It might be interesting to ask several people and see how they respond.

One way people unintentionally create their own realities is through heuristics and cognitive biases. A heuristic is a "rule of thumb" or pattern that people create to respond quickly to similar situations. A cognitive bias is a tendency to think a certain way. People adopt different heuristics and cognitive biases as shortcuts to avoid more difficult analysis and take quicker action. When they do this, they create different realities for themselves.

## WHAT I NEED TO DO

Be cognizant of people's differing views of reality.

Decide what is more expeditious: (a) helping the customer within the reality the customer has created, or (b) helping the customer see a different view. Each situation is different. Sometimes you will be able to operate easily within the customer's mental framework. In other situations you will have no choice but to show the customer evidence of another reality.

Be on the lookout for your customer's reliance on biases and heuristics that may prejudice her views. Often, once a person realizes she has used an invalid assumption, she will reformulate her conclusions.

As irrational as people's realities may seem to you, their realities are very real to them. Imagine yourself in their situations and try to see what they see. If you were that person in that situation, what would you do? Remember, the question is not what *you* would do in that situation!



## ACTION SUMMARY

- Always assume people see the same thing differently.
- Understand the logic, regardless of its soundness, used to arrive at conclusions.
- Put yourself in the other people's shoes and see what they see.

# SECRET # 41
# FORGET THE WISHFUL THINKING

*A goal without a plan is just a wish.*
*—Antoine de Saint-Exupéry*

## WHAT I NEED TO KNOW

The cognitive bias called "wishful thinking" is the tendency to consider only the data that reinforces your desired views and reject data that negates them. I am astounded at how many brilliant people and executives choose wishes over reality—to their great detriment.

Perhaps the clearest example is that of Quentin Thomas Wiles, a successful venture capitalist who invested $20 million in a company called Miniscribe in 1985. Mr. Wiles, a can-do, don't-take-no-for-an-answer kind of person, personally took command of Miniscribe in mid-1985. He earnestly wanted to grow the company to $1 billion in revenues despite an industry-wide downturn and losing its main customers, IBM, Apple, and Digital Equipment Corp. Mr. Wiles rejected any data that negated his $1 billion wish and fired executives who brought him anything but positive data. He became so feared that employees resorted to shipping bricks (the company actually made computer disk drives) to fictitious customers rather than tell Mr. Wiles the company was not on track for $1 billion.

The consequences of Mr. Wiles' wishful thinking?

- The company (and many of its suppliers) filed for bankruptcy.
- More than 5,700 people lost their jobs.
- Mr. Wiles received a criminal conviction and a three-year jail sentence.
- Mr. Wiles' career ended—in disgrace.

## WHAT I NEED TO DO

As a change leader, you do not have the luxury of wishing things to be true. Gather as much objective data as possible and provide an objective analysis to the customer. Be careful of the customer who:

- Underestimates costs or risks.
- Overestimates the benefits and chances of success.

Accurate expectations are not just in the customer's best interest—they are in your best interest.

Second, make sure that people on your delivery team are not just wishing things to happen. Foster a can-do, problem-solving culture on your team and confront problems quickly and actively. Always keep the customer apprised of status, including any problems.

Most important, do not let yourself wish. Do this by remaining emotionally detached from the situation and not becoming enmeshed with the data or the outcomes. High energy and excellence in execution is different from emotional attachment.



## ACTION SUMMARY

- Be sensitive of wishful thinking.
- Replace wishful thinking with problem solving and action.
- Avoid the dangers of wishful thinkers—by disengaging from them.

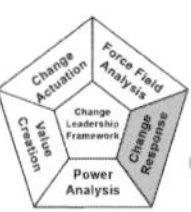


# Secret # 42
# Win with Mere Exposure

*Just as nature abhors a vacuum, humans resist change. Change will occur; vacuums will be filled.*
*—Nikki Giovanni*

## What I Need to Know

People have an incredible preference for items and situations that are familiar. People actually prefer to suffer with something familiar than change to something different.

Examples of this cognitive bias, called "mere exposure," are innumerable. One that sticks out in my mind is my father's preference for Lincoln Towncars. At one point in his life, he perceived the Lincoln Towncar as the ultimate car to own. So he has been driving Lincoln Towncars for four decades. Right now, there are two in his garage. All my life I have heard my mother complain about slick roads in Colorado. I guess I always thought she was a wimp because the snow never slowed me down. The real situation finally dawned on me recently when I was caught in an ice storm while driving a car similar to the Lincoln Towncar. It was like being on an ice-skating rink without skates. My car was useless. I had to have my wife come and pick me up in our four-wheel drive. Then, I realized my parents were not driving in the comfort of Lincoln Towncars; they were driving in the fear that results from being on an ice-skating rink with the wrong shoes. I told my parents they would have a whole new sense of freedom if they traded just one of the two Towncars for any one of a hundred other cars that would drive better in the snow. But what was their response? "Oh, we're not familiar with those. We don't need to go anywhere, anyway. We'll just stay home."

How many similar examples can you think of?

## What I Need to Do

Since you know your customer has a preference for the familiar, you need to expose your customer to the proposed changes until the customer feels familiar with them.

Put a section in your account plan called "Familiarity Tactics" and brainstorm with your team about all the ways you can improve familiarity for the various stakeholders.

Advertising agencies use the phenomena of mere exposure to their advantage, by repeating their message over...and over...and over. This not only helps people remember the product or brand, but it establishes an almost subconscious level of familiarity.

If a person has demonstrated a clear preference for familiarity, introduce new ideas gradually and gently "seed" his thinking. Then, follow up multiple times with the same idea, taking care each time not to apply any pressure, saying, for example, "Have you considered [the idea]?"



## Action Summary

- Be aware that people may prefer the familiar over the better.
- Develop specific tactics to turn "unknown" into "familiar."
- Rather than use pressure, use repetition to seed ideas for change.

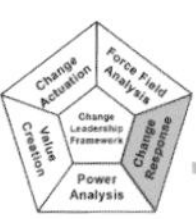


# Secret # 43
# Beware of False Consensus

*To a large degree reality is whatever the people who are around at the time agree to.*

*—Milton H. Miller*

## What I Need to Know

"False consensus" is a tendency to assume that other people share the same views. Maybe you assume they share your view. Or maybe you assume they share each others' views. Either way, the danger is that you drive down a path and suddenly realize you are alone.

A more likely scenario is that deep into the process of building a coalition of support for the change proposal, you realize there is disagreement among the coalition members regarding basic premises of the change. The resulting misunderstandings could result in rework, reduced credibility, and impaired relationships. Ultimately, the coalition could fall apart, perhaps even in acrimony.

I starkly remember one client company where a coalition member held very strong views that the rest of the members did not share. In every weekly meeting, he would make statements like "I thought we all agreed [to his view]." The coalition did not fall apart, but it never really got off the ground, either, because every week the members would have to rehash the same questions.

## WHAT I NEED TO DO

Utilize "active listening" skills to restate your understanding of each stakeholder's view in your own words. Do this for every stakeholder. And do it in writing whenever possible.

Documents are the change leader's most important tools. Seeing things in black and white helps drive clarity and commitment. Put everything in black and white and review it with the customer, starting with your very first discussion.

Each organization develops its own unique documents it uses to communicate and make decisions. Adapt to the organization's practices and use their formats. But also develop your own standard templates to demonstrate your experience and expertise.

Make sure you provide mechanisms and time for stakeholders to provide their feedback along the path. Do not always assume silence indicates agreement. Try methodically to obtain feedback or agreement from everyone, even from the quietest person in the corner. Everyone's view is important—and anyone could derail a consensus.



## ACTION SUMMARY

- Verify people's views by saying, "What I heard was..."
- Put things in black and white for people to review and agree on.
- Try to include everyone in the consensus.

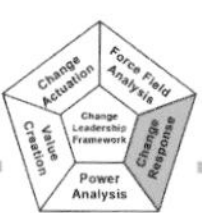


# Secret # 44
# Be Careful Where You Cast Your Anchor

*To reach a port we must sail, sometimes with the wind, and sometimes against it. But we must not drift or lie at anchor.*
*—Oliver Wendell Holmes*

## What I Need to Know

"Anchoring" is the cognitive bias whereby people are overly influenced by an initial data point, either in the past or present.

The potential trap for your customer is that she may limit herself and miss opportunities. For example, if you try a new restaurant and have a bad experience, you may vow never to go back. But what if two months later the bad manager is gone and a new manager is doing a great job? You will be missing an opportunity for a great experience because you anchored yourself to the initial data point. Fortunately, even though people are often too lazy to pursue more than one data point, they will usually be willing to consider new data if you provide it.

You can fall into the same trap as a salesperson. Maybe you determine that a customer is not able or willing to make certain changes. Then, you write that customer off your list and never go back. But what happens if two months later that person is gone and a new manager is in? The opportunity goes to your competitor.

Another trap for you is setting initial customer expectations. If you sheepishly lowball your initial cost estimates, the customer will be anchored to that number; it may be nearly impossible for you to raise the cost when you inevitably realize the actual cost is much higher.

## What I Need to Do

A common practice among salespeople is to bait the customer with an initial low price and then switch to a much higher price, later. The ethics of this practice are debatable. But as much as I hate to admit it, this practice has been proven to work. In *Forceful Selling*, I talked about my house painter initially quoting me a price of $35 per hour and then coming back with thousands and thousands of dollars of invoices. He didn't do anything unethical—the hours just add up fast. (By the way, I have written two books—and he is still there! He's getting paid by the hour, after all.)

Sometimes, you may want to consider making your proposal two or three times bigger than your initial estimates would indicate—just be sure to justify it with objective data. This has the effect of anchoring the customer's expectations at a much higher price, making the ultimate price seem relatively small and achievable. This tactic is standard practice for tort attorneys who initially ask for tens of millions of dollars in damages, hoping to bias a jury toward a higher judgment in the end.



## Action Summary

- Be aware of the perils and opportunities created by anchoring.
- Use anchoring as a tool.
- Do not pay your painter by the hour!

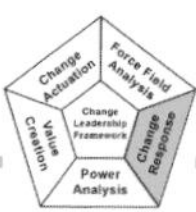


# SECRET # 45
# MARATHONS ARE AEROBIC

*Fill the unforgiving minute with*
*sixty seconds' worth of distance run.*
—*Rudyard Kipling*

## WHAT I NEED TO KNOW

There is a bias called the "sustainability bias," whereby a person comes to believe that extreme performance can be sustained, rather than regressing to the normal, sustainable level.

Managers are especially susceptible to asking people for extraordinary effort and then expecting them to maintain it indefinitely. The result is premature exhaustion of resources, otherwise known as "burnout." The danger for the manager is to commit to a schedule that cannot be achieved without sustained extraordinary effort. The manager gets farther and farther behind in her commitments and continues to request ever-increasing levels of extraordinary effort. Ultimately, the manager may fail to meet her commitments and lose responsibility for the project (and even go to jail). I could mention many names that have recently been in the news, but will only remind you of Q. T. Wiles from Miniscribe.

This is not just a Wall Street phenomenon. You and your customer are susceptible to it also. Have you had a customer who expected you to jump through flaming hoops? Have you worked like crazy to make your revenue targets only to have a higher target the next time? Or maybe you have asked your team to work extra hard to deliver commitments you made to the customer?

You and your customers are in a marathon. Marathon runners steadily burn a supply of oxygen and energy—it is an aerobic sport. Sprinting is anaerobic. Sprinters don't use oxygen—but they stop after one hundred meters.

## What I Need to Do

Take care to undercommit and overdeliver as much as possible.

One definition of quality is "meeting customer expectations." Therefore, to deliver high quality, you must be diligent in setting expectations that you can exceed.

Avoid the common mistake of not including allowances for risk. Experienced contractors know the costs of risk. My painter refuses to work on a project basis; he prefers a time-and-materials-based price. He says, "If I quote you a piece price, I'm going to have to factor in a whole lot of risk and you're not going to like the price." The real issue is that he is not willing to share any risk. You will not have happy customers if you ask them to take all the risk. Conversely, you will not have any profits if you take all the risk.

Remember, you are in a marathon. Work hard, but do not expect yourself or others to perform "unnatural acts."

Rather than relying on extraordinary effort, rely on extraordinary planning and discipline—they make extraordinary execution.



## Action Summary

- Beware of unsustainable expectations.
- Undercommit and overdeliver.
- Risk is real—make sure you allow for it.

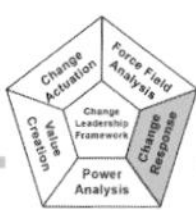


# Secret # 46
# Don't Be Deluded by Illusions

*Life consists not in holding good cards, but in playing well those you do hold.*

*—Josh Billings*

## What I Need to Know

The control illusion bias is the tendency to overestimate one's ability to control outcomes and the factors that influence them, such as other people's behaviors.

A potential trap is that a person may take action based on certain assumptions of other people's behaviors or other events. This is called "taking a dependency." In other words, the person's outcome is dependent on the actions of others. If the other events do not occur, or the other people fail to act as anticipated, then the person may experience a "suboptimal outcome," (i.e., fail miserably).

While it may sound obvious that you cannot control other people, we lose sight of this every day. In fact, there are terms that encourage the illusion of control. In sales, there is the term "account control." And in the legal profession, there is the term "client control." Sales managers and judges use these terms, respectively, to refer to the salesperson and attorney's ability to manage the client's behavior.

Customers also can be deluded by illusions of control. How many times have you heard the refrain, "I have it under control"? Customers may erroneously believe a change is unnecessary because everything is "under control." Conversely, they may overestimate their influence over resources and attempt to drive change that is too big to be achieved with the actual amount of committed resources.

## WHAT I NEED TO DO

Be cognizant of your client's perception of control. Always try to validate her assumptions with other people. Do other people point you to that person saying, "You have to talk to her. What she says, goes"? Or when you ask who is responsible, do they say, "That's kind of complicated. There are several organizations involved"?

Be very thorough in identifying, clarifying, and documenting dependencies. Take a project manager's view and identify owners and completion dates for all dependencies. Be sure to suggest contingencies and risk mitigation plans for each.

Remember, the discipline of change response analysis is about characterizing the customer's behaviors. So test the customer's assumptions and behaviors regularly. Does the customer step up in meetings and take control? Or does he quickly back down when challenged? If he tells you something will happen, or someone will agree to his request, does it come true?

Finally, do not delude yourself. You cannot control the customer. But you can characterize the customer.



## ACTION SUMMARY

- Validate all claims of control and influence.
- Identify all dependencies and their mitigations.
- Characterize the customer's behavior under various conditions.

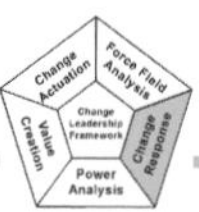


# SECRET # 47
# DOUBLE YOUR BEST ESTIMATE

*Projects are like armies; never approach them without twice the resources.*

*—Brett Clay*

## WHAT I NEED TO KNOW

The planning fallacy is the tendency to underestimate significantly the number of resources required to complete a task. Studies show that even expert estimates, utilizing "bottom-up" analysis of work breakdown structures, underestimate actual resource utilization by 70 percent. In other words, the actual resource requirements are, on average, 1.7 times the original estimate.

One potential trap is that a person undertakes a project and exhausts available resources before completing the project and achieving the desired result. To make matters worse, the person may rely on the denial coping strategy and attempt to squeeze more output from insufficient resources, often referred to as "squeezing blood from a turnip." Of course, this rarely works and the person has a high probability of failure.

A similar trap is that the person underestimates the resources required to maintain the status quo. In this case, the person should have changed to a lower-cost course, but he also fails to achieve his goals due to insufficient resources.

Successful executives develop a track record of achieving their goals. They do this by "sand-bagging" their commitments. In other words, they make sure any commitment is reinforced by many factors that ensure their ability to meet the commitment.

## WHAT I NEED TO DO

The most obvious way to put sandbags around your commitments is to double your best estimate of required resources (1.7 times to be exact). This may seem like a bitter pill. And you may scare some customers. But the data does not lie. The average project goes over budget by at least 1.7 times.

Another common way of dealing with the extra 70 percent is to clearly specify descriptions and ownership of deliverables and risks in the contract. Then, any variance requires a change order; a new order in effect.

If you are in the contracting business, then you are likely already very familiar with these processes. The point to remember as a change leader is that customers tend to underestimate almost everything—from the pain and cost of the status quo to the resources required to make a change, to the benefits of making the change. This problem can trip you up in many ways. So, be aware of them and watch where you step.



## ACTION SUMMARY

- Continually ask, "What happens if this requires twice the resources?" Then prepare for it.
- Share, rather than take the risk.
- Double check all estimates; then double them.

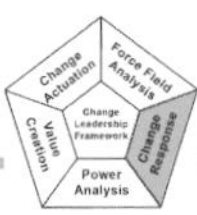

# SECRET # 48
# THE GLORY DAYS NEVER WERE

*No man can prove upon awakening that he is the man who he thinks went to sleep the night before, or that anything that he recollects is anything other than a convincing dream.*
*—R. Buckminster Fuller*

## WHAT I NEED TO KNOW

The rosy retrospection bias is the tendency to remember past events in a more positive light than they were experienced. For example, "It wasn't that painful to have our first child—let's have another!"

A number of perils can befall people when they consider the past. First, if a person "undervalues" the extent of resources, effort, and pain that were expended and experienced in the past, then the person may under-estimate the cost of repeating the event in the future. Thus, the person may undertake the effort with insufficient resources and fail in the execution. Another risk is that the person, using erroneous cost assumptions, may reject better alternatives, thereby missing an opportunity.

A person can also have recollections that are more negative than the events really were. The person may then, without proper consideration, reject a similar idea in the future, thereby missing an opportunity to enhance his business or life.

It is important to remember that people's memories of the past are influenced by many situational factors. For example, a person suffering from a head cold may have a bad memory of a movie she watched in a movie theater. Another example is how good trail mix tastes after four hours of hiking up a mountain. Try eating trail mix after eating dinner and desert. It doesn't taste quite as good.

## WHAT I NEED TO DO

Always be suspicious of people's recollections of the past. They are rarely accurate—they are either biased too negatively or too positively.

Attempt to collect objective assessments of the past by asking for quantifiable and verifiable data whenever possible.

Attempt to make assessments of the status quo and possible future changes without relying on past data. Substantiate these estimates with current data.

If you must rely to some degree on past data, try to uncover any situational factors that may bias the data. Not only can the past situation bias the past data, but the current situation could be a source of bias. For example, a person may currently be under pressure and, in his desperation, start wishing data to be true, rather than proving data to be true.



## ACTION SUMMARY

- Be suspicious of past data and be sure to validate it.
- Uncover situational factors that may bias past data.
- Try to use current data whenever possible.

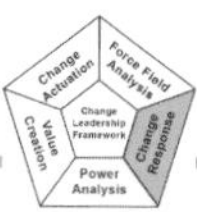


# SECRET # 49
# CHOOSE CHANGES WISELY

*To wish to progress is the largest part of progress.*
*—Lucius Annaeus Seneca (1st century A.D.)*

## WHAT I NEED TO KNOW

Once a person has coped with the forces in her life space and has either removed or is operating within the constraints of her cognitive biases, she must form a view of her change space. In other words, she must develop a set of possible changes and select one. There are many ways to model the change space in organizations. The change leader will need to pick the model that is most applicable to the organization and situation under consideration.

One model that is instructive is the Four Forces of the Change Leadership Framework, depicted by the illustration on the opposite page. The three arrows represent three forces: environmental factors, behavioral tendencies, and cognitive strategies. The triangle in the middle represents two concepts.

First, it represents the force of internal needs and serves as a reminder of Maslow's Hierarchy of Needs, starting at the bottom with physiological needs and rising to the pinnacle of the triangle with self-actualization. The triangle is at the center of the diagram to indicate that internal needs play the central role in a person's life space. This is further emphasized by the three arrows circling the triangle.

The other idea represented by the triangle is the Greek letter Delta, which symbolizes "change" in mathematics. So the triangle also reminds us that the Four Forces are always driving change.

Use the Four Forces Model to develop a list of possible changes and then to weigh the tradeoffs.

## What I Need to Do

First, make sure you have characterized the customer's change response such that you have a good understanding of the person's change capacity and behaviors.

Then, help the customer develop a set of possible ways of responding to the forces he feels. It might be insightful to think of the various options as plane tickets having points of departure, destinations, prices, and availability.

For each option, determine the changes in each dimension of the Four Forces model that will be required to support the change. Also, there is a fifth dimension that should not be overlooked—changing the cognitive structure, which means changing the person's perception of the force, rather than the force itself.

As the customer considers the various options, try to help the customer visualize the new situation as if watching a movie. Many people do not bother to "see" how the movie ends and then select options with less than ideal outcomes. Help your customer play the movie to the end and to choose options with good endings.



## Action Summary

- Map out the change options.
- Determine forces required to support each option.
- Visualize the change as a movie and "play" the movie to the end.

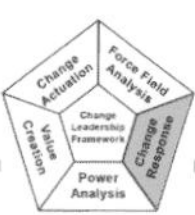


# SECRET # 50
# CHANGE PATHS TO SUCCESS

*My great concern is not whether you have failed, but whether you are content with your failure.*

*—Abraham Lincoln*

## WHAT I NEED TO KNOW

How many successful football running backs put their heads down and run in a straight line? Successful running backs keep their heads up and continually change paths in response to events as they unfold.

When a path gets to a dead end, don't despair; get on a different path. If a path were certain, then the path would already have been taken. So the change leader and her client must acknowledge the risks that accompany any change. The reason you or your client are currently considering making a change is because, in one way or another, the current path is not working. If, after getting on the next path, it does not work either, then you will simply need to do it again.

Of course, no one wants to be a Chicken, constantly changing directions before giving each change a chance to succeed. But neither do you want to be like the chicken that was born in a large poultry farm and watched every day as thousands of frozen chickens were taken to the market. Outside the gargantuan chicken coop, a road led out of the farm. Do you know why the chicken crossed the road? He figured he wasn't really crossing it. He was just going to the other side of the same road—the road to the market. The chicken was fried the next day. Success requires being willing to change to entirely different paths, and then following through and giving the new path a chance to succeed.

## What I Need to Do

It's one thing if you are the person changing paths. But what should you do to get the customer to change paths?

The first step is to ask the customer to play out in his mind where the current path is leading. If he prefers to cope by refusing to acknowledge the current path is leading to an undesirable outcome, you will have to keep checking back with the customer until the inevitable day comes when he confronts reality.

The second step is to ask the customer if he had a magic time machine and could magically jump into the ideal future, what would it be?

The last step is to ask the customer to walk backward from the ideal situation to the current situation, asking, "What has to change for this to happen?" each step along the way.

Many people are anxious of uncertainty along a different path. Ask the person, "How certain is the current path?" Then, remind him that uncertain hope is better than certain failure.



## Action Summary

- Success often requires changing paths.
- Objectively assess the expected outcome of the current path.
- Determine what events must happen along the path to success.

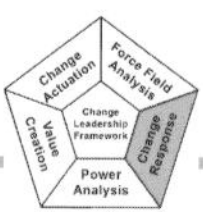


# SECRET # 51
# NO PAIN, NO GAIN

*Genius is the infinite capacity for taking pains.*
*—Jane Ellis Hopkins*

## WHAT I NEED TO KNOW

Change involves risk—the risks of making the change and the risks of not changing. But change also has cost. One of the costs of change is pain. Change may not be easy. It may be downright difficult and painful. That does not mean it is not necessary. For example, is it easy for geese to move their entire flock across continents? Geese burn a massive amount of calories and endure significant hardships moving over such great distances. But if they did not do it, they would perish.

My image of pain is watching riders in the Tour de France ride hundreds of miles a day for three weeks, seemingly straight up and down mountains. I try to do an hour of spin cycling at least three times a week. If you have taken a spinning class, then you know how painful it is. It is hard to imagine, while on the spinning bike, that the Tour de France riders do it for six hours a day, every day. I figure if Lance Armstrong can do it faster than anyone, seven times in a row, and beat cancer, then we can endure the pain of a little change in our life spaces.

No one should expect change to be painless. Rather, everyone should expect to understand the forces driving change and to harness them effectively.

## What I Need to Do

Change is serious business—take it seriously.

Change is painful business—take pains to minimize the costs.

Change is risky business—take actions to reduce or eliminate risks.

Carefully set expectations. Set realistic expectations for the benefits to be realized by changing. And set realistic expectations for the costs of changing.

Remind your client that just as "there is no free lunch," it is not realistic to expect gain without some amount of pain. If the customer has rational expectations, setting these expectations will help you underpromise and overdeliver. If the person is scared off by these expectations, then his expectations are irrational; you may want to consider disengaging from a customer who will be difficult and costly to satisfy.



## Action Summary

- Carefully set expectations.
- Avoid painting impossibly rosy scenarios that set the customer up for disappointment.
- Underpromise and overdeliver.

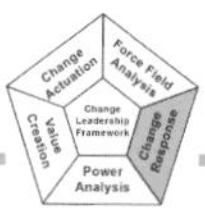

# SECRET # 52
# THERE IS NO MAGIC

*Everyone prefers belief to the exercise of judgment.*
*—Lucius Annaeus Seneca (1st century A.D)*

## WHAT I NEED TO KNOW

This secret is a reminder to continually characterize the Jack-in-the-box and the various stakeholders' change responses.

Remember the stories of Harry Houdini, the famous magician and escape artist from the early twentieth century? Houdini entertained people for many years with his "magical" escape acts. He apparently felt this was all good fun and entertainment for his audiences. But when a group of people started to gain fame by claiming they could "channel" communications from deceased loved ones, he felt the people who were led to believe they were talking to their deceased loved ones were being exploited and harmed. As a magician, Houdini knew all the tricks being employed by the "channelers." He became incensed and worked feverishly to expose the fraud.

This may sound heretical, but a change leader needs to be a skeptic—just as Houdini the magician was skeptical of magic. To be a successful change leader you must be extremely trustworthy. Otherwise, people simply will not follow your lead.

When people say things that sound too good to be true, or the plan of record calls for "magic happens here," be very, very careful what you are getting into. Your trustworthiness will be tarnished if you become associated with empty facts or empty results. (I hope it goes without saying that, for the same reasons, you should not perpetrate "magic" yourself.)

## WHAT I NEED TO DO

Develop your "brand identity" as a person with the following qualities:

- Voice of reality
- Common ground found here
- Results happen here
- Truth—like it or not
- Progress—not regress
- It's not easy—but it's worth it

To avoid "magical" surprises, Jacks popping out the box, being sent on "wild goose chases" or just simple miscommunications, you should diligently seek to improve your understanding of the force fields of each stakeholder. To use spy terms, you should continually collect intelligence and maintain a psychological dossier of all stakeholders. What are each person's internal needs? How do they tend to behave? How do they tend to cope? What strategies do they rely on? What have been their change responses in similar situations in the past? How is the current situation different? and so on.



## ACTION SUMMARY

- Be skeptical at all times.
- Never tarnish your trustworthiness.
- Be "intelligent"—know what is up the magician's sleeve.

# Secret # 53
# Don't Blow a Gasket

*The world belongs to the enthusiast who keeps cool.*
*—William McFee*

## What I Need to Know

During the twentieth century, Norman Vincent Peale was considered one of the most influential evangelists of the power of a positive mental attitude. Taking a more scientific approach, Kurt Lewin also cited research that showed people who perceived an ability to control outcomes reported a higher level of satisfaction with the outcomes than those who perceived a lack of control.

I am sure I am "preaching to the choir" when I mention the need for a change leader to be motivational and to inspire stakeholders to embrace and implement change. The change leader must be the stabilizing influence who always maintains a positive mental attitude. However, the change leader must couch her positive mental attitude and enthusiasm with a certain level of detachment and the constant awareness that she is the agent of change, not the cause or the driving force of the change.

In *The Fifth Discipline*, Peter Senge talks about advocacy versus inquiry as he describes the characteristics of a learning organization, that is, an organization with a high capacity for change. In the Change Leadership Framework, the change leader's primary role is that of inquirer—inquiring into the forces that influence the person or the organization. The change leader's secondary role is that of the advocate—advocating the changes and resulting outcomes desired by the client.

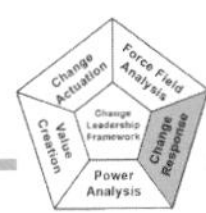




## What I Need to Do

You, the change leader, must do all of this—maintain a positive mental attitude, be inspirational, be an advocate, be an agent employed by the client—all while remaining emotionally detached and objective. As soon as the change leader becomes emotionally enmeshed with the change proposals, he loses objectivity, perceptiveness, effectiveness, and credibility—he has become one of the stakeholders on the playing field, rather than the "invisible hand" that guides stakeholders to their desired outcomes.

Go ahead and inquire into the benefits of changing. Go ahead and play back the client's vision of how beautiful things will be after the change is made. Go ahead and be an advocate of reason and an engine of action. Just be mindful of the boundaries of the engine's cylinder and pressure. Don't blow a gasket and blow up the change initiative by overstepping these bounds.



## Action Summary

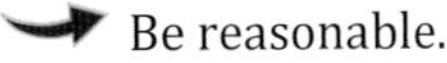

- Be reasonable.
- Be supportive.
- Be detached.

# SECRET # 54
# SHORT CUTS = SHORT CIRCUITS

*Patience is bitter, but its fruit is sweet.*
*—Jean Jacques Rousseau*

## WHAT I NEED TO KNOW

Have you ever short-circuited an electrical wire? When you short-circuit a wire, it either blows a fuse or starts a fire. Either way, the electricity goes out and everything stops working until things are fixed. That's an appropriate way to think about what will happen if you try to take a shortcut in the change process. What seems like a way to speed things up at the time can end up not only taking longer, but it can also cause significant damage that can take a long while to fix, if the damage is reparable at all.

A successful change leader must be highly disciplined. An extremely successful change leader must be extremely disciplined.

What is discipline? Discipline is adhering to order.

Successful change leaders have a well-organized, systematic approach to driving change—and they adhere to it.

A couple years ago, I was in Denver, Colorado, for a conference and I took in a game of baseball with some friends. In the bottom of the ninth inning, Brad Hawpe of the Colorado Rockies was at bat, down five runs to six, with two outs and two strikes. The Rockies were one swing away from losing—only a home run on the last swing could save the game. Incredibly, Hawpe hit a homer into the center stands! The Rockies won seven to six in the eleventh inning. It was amazing!!

Yes, one-in-a-million miracles can happen. But do you want to be successful one out of a million times, or do you want to succeed every time?

## WHAT I NEED TO DO

Change is like a fragile house of cards that must be carefully built, one card at a time, in a certain order.

Do not succumb to the temptation of taking a short cut, or doing something out of order, before its time has come.

You will always be under pressure, particularly from your management, to speed things along and may even be encouraged to take short cuts. Ask yourself and your management, "Do I want it done right (resulting in a purchase order), or right now (resulting in a lost opportunity)?" Many times the question becomes, "Do I want the purchase order later—or never?"

That is not an excuse for sitting by the phone expecting an order magically to come in. On the contrary, as a disciplined change leader, you have a well-organized, systematic approach that you have to create and execute. You have roadblocks to remove, risks to mitigate, a coalition to energize...the list goes on. So, put down this book and get to work!



## ACTION SUMMARY

- Be extremely disciplined—and be extremely successful.
- Be disciplined—adhere to order.
- Get the order later, rather than never.

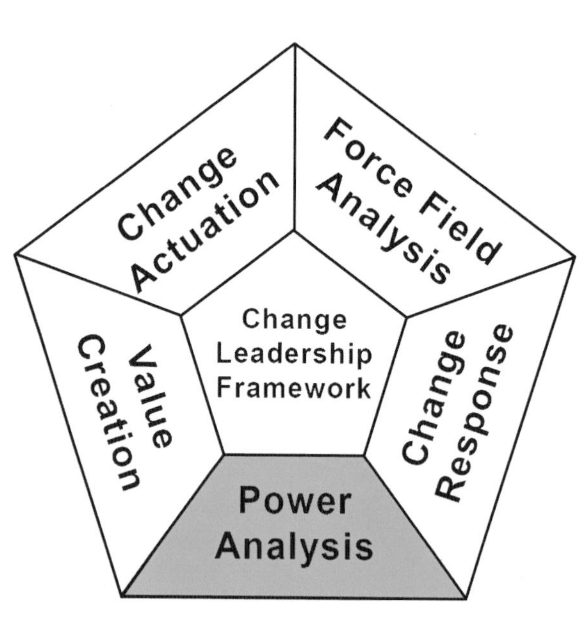
Change Actuation
Force Field Analysis
Change Leadership Framework
Value Creation
Change Response
Power Analysis

# POWER ANALYSIS

## THE THIRD DISCIPLINE

# INTRODUCTION

## TO

# POWER ANALYSIS

---

### What is it?

Power analysis is the process of assessing the effort required to make a change.

Making a change involves:

- Breaking free of the current situation
- Overcoming resisting forces
- Moving from the current situation to the new situation
- Maintaining the new situation in place

The discipline of power analysis assesses these efforts.

### Why is it important?

Before a change can be implemented, it must be planned, budgeted and approved. Evaluating the various implementation strategies and choosing the lowest cost option is a critical step for successfully implementing the change.

### How is it new or different?

The traditional sales approach is to develop an estimate of time and materials, possibly including a project plan, and then obtain support from a powerful executive. The Change Leadership Framework prescribes a more proactive leadership role, whereby the salesperson develops a detailed understanding of the driving

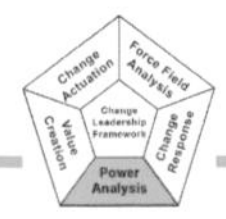




and resisting forces in the organization or the individual person's life. The salesperson then seeks to reinforce the driving forces and reduce the resisting forces, giving the change initiative the best chance of success.

## What are the common misconceptions?

People typically think of the process of making change as having the power to make people do something they don't want to do. Even the concept of "change management" practiced by human resource and organizational development professionals is essentially the process of implementing an executive decision by taking employees through the Kubler-Ross Five-Stages-of-Grief model. Could you imagine walking into a customer and saying, "Look, I've decided you are all going to change. You may not like it, but you'll just have to get over it. You can cry if you like. But, eventually you'll accept it when you realize you still have a job."? That might be change management, but it certainly is not change leadership!

Change leadership is helping people overcome the power required to achieve their goals. Astute change leaders seek to lower the power requirements, thereby lowering the difficulty of making the change.

## What are the key take-aways & how do I put them in action?

Don't just rely on "selling to power" to obtain order approval and implementation. Add more value to the executive by understanding all of the forces in the organization and providing leadership to make the change successful.

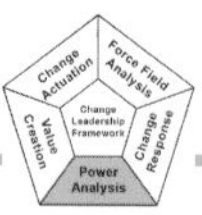


# SECRET # 55
# UNDERSTAND THE EFFORT

*It isn't the mountains ahead that wear you out.*
*It's the grain of sand in your shoe.*
*—Anonymous*

## WHAT I NEED TO KNOW

Power may be associated with many things, but in the Change Leadership Framework, power is a measure of effort. Physicists define power as the amount of work performed over time.

$$Power = \frac{work}{time}$$

If one change requires two months working every day to complete and another change requires one month working every day, then the first change requires twice the power. Another way to think about it is if both changes were to be completed in one month, then the first change would require twice as much power.

The unit of measure for power is a "watt." A change that requires a lot of effort could be referred to as a "high-wattage change." For example, the electrical power generated by the Hoover Dam on the Colorado River is about two thousand megawatts. So when your boss assigns you a new project, you could say, "Oh, that's a Hooverwatt change! We'll have to harness the power of the Colorado River to accomplish that!" Or you could say, "Oh, that's a megawattage project—I'm going to need a megaraise to complete that." When you think a change will be easy, you could say, "No problem. That's a milliwatt (a milliwatt is a thousandth of a watt). A firefly could generate that much power. I'll have it done in a millisecond."

## What I Need to Do

As you help the customer choose a course of action and begin to formulate a plan, estimating the power required to make the proposed changes becomes imperative.

Estimate the power by breaking down the work into packages that can be individually estimated. Whenever possible, solicit estimates from experts in the particular area, or better yet, the people who would actually do the work. Then, sum the estimates of the individual work packages.

A unit of measure analogous to watts might be person-months per month. Of course, the ultimate measure of the cost of a change is the amount of dollars spent. But a simple dollar amount does not reflect whether the dollars are used in a year or a month. Even a measure that accounts for time, such as net present value, does not account for important indirect costs such as the opportunity cost of scarce resources. Early in the decision making, rough order-of-magnitude estimates will suffice. As the project gets closer to actuation—and contract—much more accurate estimates will be required.

## Action Summary

- Estimate power required as work over a period of time.
- Use previous projects or "bottom-up" estimates as guides.
- Refer to your Force Fan Out Map (discussed on page 79) to consider indirect costs.

# SECRET # 56
# UNDERSTAND THE SCALES OF CHANGE

*Action is a lack of balance.*

*—James A. Baldwin*

## WHAT I NEED TO KNOW

As we discussed in Section 3, Force Field Analysis, every force has an opposing force, which Lewin called a "restraining" force, or "resisting" force. Lewin said that a person is in equilibrium if the driving and restraining forces are equal, and the person would be in motion if the driving force is larger than the restraining force. In other words, change happens when driving forces outweigh opposing (restraining) forces. The figure on the opposite page illustrates the concept of the Scales of Change. If the equilibrium is disturbed and the driving forces outweigh resisting forces, the scale will tip and change will occur. It is interesting to note that only a small additional amount may tip the scale.

It is also important to note that when many people think of force field analysis, they think of the Scales of Change, represented by the simple equation:

$$f\{driving\ forces\} \geq f\{resisting\ forces\}$$

However, in the Change Leadership Framework, force field analysis refers to the process of independently assessing the forces on each side of the scale—the Four Forces.

$$\begin{aligned}&Driving\ \&\ Resisting\ Forces\\&= f\{Needs, Behaviors, Strategies, Environment\}\end{aligned}$$

Therefore, in the Change Leadership Framework, the power analysis discipline is where we compare the results of the force field analysis, weighing driving forces versus resisting forces.

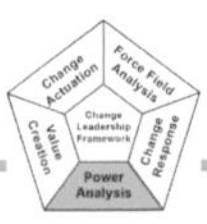



## What I Need to Do

The first step in assessing the effort required to make a change is to perform a thorough force field analysis of the driving and resisting forces. A minimum force field analysis identifies at least 1 force in each of the Four Forces dimensions for both the drivers and resistors, for a minimum of 4 driving forces and 4 resisting forces. A thorough analysis would identify 3 to 5 forces in each of the Four Forces dimensions, for a total of 12 to 20 driving forces and 12 to 20 resisting forces. You will find that brainstorming 20 forces is actually fairly easy. You will also find that you will discover valuable new insights into the situation when you do this.

The next step is to assess the effort associated with each force. For example, if one of the resisting forces is some kind of habitual behavior, you would estimate the effort required to manage the behavior and its collateral costs. To weigh the efforts on each side of the scale, you will need apples-to-apples comparisons of the various efforts. Either convert all the estimates to a common unit of measure, such as "person-months per month," or use a scale from, say, 1 to 5, to assess the relative efforts.



## Action Summary

- Perform a more thorough force field analysis to increase the accuracy of the power analysis.
- Be sure to use apples-to-apples comparisons.
- Remember that the quantities are not as important as the insights gained by performing the analysis.

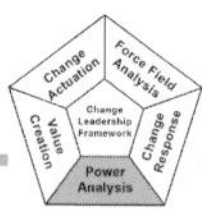


# SECRET # 57
# QUALIFY THE RESISTANCE

*A problem adequately stated is a problem well on its way to being solved.*

*—R. Buckminster Fuller*

## WHAT I NEED TO KNOW

People usually associate making changes with overcoming resistance. By now, you understand that every driving force has a resisting force and that any attempt at change will be met with resistance. Let's look at some common sources of resistance:

**Habits/homeostasis**. Most people have a natural preference for keeping things as they are now and how they always have been.

**Lack of familiarity**. People seem to have a universal preference for things they know and understand.

**Beneficiary of the status quo**. Stakeholders who are benefitting quite handsomely in the current situation may fiercely resist changing the situation.

**Conflicting goals**. If a stakeholder has a different goal, that is, he is influenced by a different set of forces or has a different view of them, then he may resist the change.

**Zero-sum game**. Some people may hold the notion that if one person benefits, the others lose. Not wanting to lose, they resist.

**Close-mindedness**. Some people are simply not willing to listen to new ideas.

**Anxieties**. You know someone is operating based on anxieties when appeals to logic do not seem to work.

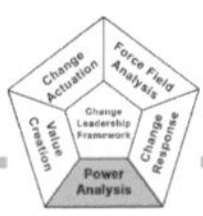



## What I Need to Do

The first steps for handling resistance are:

**Characterize the change response.** As you characterize people, remember that you are characterizing their behavior. Your primary concern is to predict their actions. Will they proactively support the change in the next big stakeholder meeting? Will they passively support it and give a weak endorsement only if called on? If they are put under pressure, will they cover their neck or yours?

**Speak softly and carry a big stick**. What is the "big stick" that a change leader can carry? It is the support of the people who have the power to make the change happen. Remember the Change Leadership Framework definition of power: the effort required to carry out the change. The change leader must have the support of the people who have the resources to execute the change.

**Disengage.** Every experienced salesperson understands the concept of disqualifying a prospect and moving on. The change leader needs to assess critically the power of the resisting forces, such as a person's stubborn close-mindedness, and determine whether the best strategy is to invest the resources elsewhere.



## Action Summary

- Identify sources of resistance.
- Shore up your support.
- Remember, action is what counts.

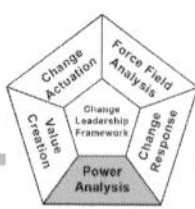


# SECRET # 58
# ESTIMATE THE RESISTANCE POWER

*The man who is swimming against*
*the stream knows the strength of it.*
*—Woodrow Wilson*

## WHAT I NEED TO KNOW

An important factor that influences the power required to make a change is the power required to overcome the resisting forces.

Here is a process for estimating the power of the resisting forces:

1. Identify resisting forces
2. Qualitatively assess the resisting forces (who, what, why, where, when, how)
3. Define scenarios for how the resistors might respond
4. Estimate the effort the resisting forces are willing and able to expend in each scenario
5. Determine the duration of the resistance

Calculate the resistance power in each scenario by multiplying the effort times the duration.

Once you have an assessment of the resistance power, you must decide how to handle the resistance. Three generic approaches are:

1. **Through**. Work through/within the constraints defined by the resisting forces.
2. **Around**. Work outside and around the boundaries the resistance cares about.
3. **Over**. Take the resistance front-on and go right over it.

## WHAT I NEED TO DO

Estimate the power of resistance keeping in mind that power can be thought of as:

- **Work over time**—How much work will the resistance expend? For how long?
- **Force times distance over time**—How far will the resistance be willing to go? For how long?
- **Force times velocity**—With what force will the resistance act? How fast?

Determine the best approach for handling the resistance: through, around, or over.

Remember the customer herself may have conflicting thoughts, such as anxieties or lack of familiarity, that provide resistance. You will need to deal systematically with each source of resistance.

Remain detached and stay off the playing field/battlefield in the organization. You may want the order, and you are the customer's agent, but the change is not your war. It is the customer's.

## ACTION SUMMARY

- Identify all sources of resistance.
- Estimate the effort the resistance will expend.
- Do not become "involved" in the change.

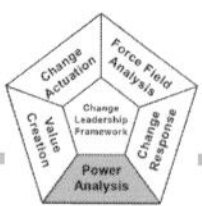


# SECRET # 59
# REDUCE TENSION

*The most important thing about power*
*is to make sure you don't have to use it.*
*—Edwin Land*

## WHAT I NEED TO KNOW

Remember that Kurt Lewin defines tension as the sum of the driving forces and the resisting forces. Also recall that every force has an equal and opposite force. So if you increase the driving force, the resistance increases—and all you've achieved is more tension. Nothing else has changed.

If the driving forces are truly overwhelming, then you could drive the change right over the resistance. In *The Art of War,* Sun Tzu says the forces have to be at least five to one, if not ten to one, before overwhelming the opponent can be safely attempted.

But, Sun Tzu pragmatically says, "The skillful leader subdues the enemy's troops without any fighting; he captures their cities without laying siege to them, he overthrows their kingdom without lengthy operations in the field." He continues, "Military tactics are like water; for water in its natural course runs away from high places (the opponent's strengths) and hastens downwards (to the opponent's weaknesses)." In change leadership, the high and low places are areas of high resistance and low resistance.

In *The Prince,* Machiavelli wrote about princes who eliminated resistance—literally.

So, it seems there is general agreement among great leaders and scholars—reducing tension by reducing both the driving and resisting forces is far more effective and efficient than attempting to overpower the resistance.

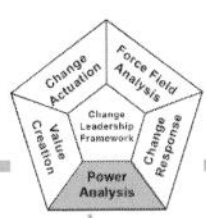




## What I Need to Do

First, understand the resisting forces both qualitatively and quantitatively.

Then, try to reduce or eliminate resisting forces one by one. For example, if a stakeholder is reluctant to change because of perceived risks, find ways to mitigate or reduce the risks down to acceptable levels. Or if people are resisting because of a lack of familiarity, communicate and, if possible, demonstrate the new situation. Do it over and over until they say, "Okay, that's enough! I get it."

Next, try to work within or around the "high places,"—areas of high resistance. Ultimately, this may require plain old compromising.

Finally, the remaining resistance will simply have to be overcome. Make sure the resources required to make the change are fully committed and are fully capable of making the change, despite the resistance.

## Action Summary

- Reduce both resisting and driving forces.
- Work "through" and "around" areas of high resistance.
- As the last resort, align power to overcome remaining resistance.

# Secret # 60
# Become a Kung-Fu Master

*Patience and time do more than strength or passion.*
*—Jean de la Fontaine (17th century)*

## What I Need to Know

When I was looking to get into sales, I heard a constant drumbeat from hiring managers who said they were only interested in hiring experienced salespeople. So, I wondered, how will I be different as a salesperson after ten years compared to my first year? I asked experienced salespeople what they thought was different and they all said the same thing. A new salesperson has lots of energy, like an excited hound dog looking under every bush for the prize. But the inexperienced salesperson's energy is largely wasted. Let's say his efficiency is about fifty percent. The experienced salesperson is incredibly deceiving. It appears as though he is moving slowly and casually. But actually the experienced salesperson keenly observes the situation, deftly sorts through all the overwhelming activities and information, and determines the one or two key issues, as well as the exact moment, that will determine the fate of the order. Perhaps that moment is ninety days from now. In the meantime, the salesperson spends the next eighty-nine days on the proverbial golf course. It looks like he is doing nothing. But he is actually eighty-nine times more efficient.

I call this phenomenon the "Kung-Fu master." When you watch a Kung-Fu master, you can barely see him move—and it's not because he is faster than lightning. It's because he really isn't moving. Yet, with a simple movement of a hand or a finger, he places an attacking black-belt instructor face down on the mat.

Sun Tzu says, "What the ancients called a clever fighter is one who not only wins, but excels in winning with ease."

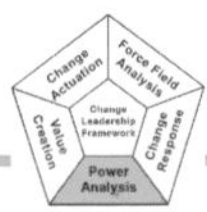



## What I Need to Do

The Kung-Fu master's strength lies not in his ability to move mountains, but to avoid tension.

Strive to reduce tension and become as efficient and effective as a Kung-Fu master by doing as the Kung-Fu master does:

- Prepare, prepare, prepare
- Assess the situation
- Know the actions people will take
- Know when your opportunity will come
- Wait patiently for the opportunity
- When the opportunity arrives, act with lightning speed!

Another characteristic of Kung-Fu masters is discipline. They faithfully prepare for all possible scenarios. They practice, practice, and practice their ability to respond in each scenario. Then, when actually in the arena, they also demonstrate the discipline to remain calm and patient in the face of crazed adversaries.



## Action Summary

- Use your energy and resources wisely.
- Wait for the right opportunity—then strike like a cobra.
- Prepare, prepare, prepare.

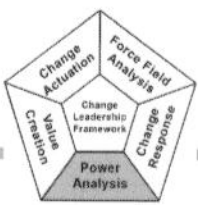


# SECRET # 61
# BE FAST AND AGILE

*Everything comes to him who hustles while he waits.*
*—Thomas Edison*

## WHAT I NEED TO KNOW

It is hard to imagine a person more physically powerful than Cortez Kennedy, an eight-time Pro-Bowl defensive tackle for the Seattle Seahawks. But guess what happened when Kennedy became known for his power. He was double- and triple-teamed. If you are not familiar with football terminology, it means the other team put two and three guys on top of him. He did not just have to overpower one 300-pound offensive lineman; he had to overpower 900 pounds of offensive linemen. The more powerful he became, the more resistance he faced and the more tension was created. All his power was essentially useless. How did he respond? He responded with speed and adaptability. Before the offensive linemen realized what was happening, their quarterback was on his back.

As change leaders, we can learn from the Cortez Kennedy playbook. Speed and adaptability can be extremely effective ways to reduce tension. There was no tension between Kennedy and the offensive linemen because the linemen were blocking his shadow. The best use of Kennedy's power was when he did not have to use it.

There is one key difference between change leadership and this football analogy, though. In football, Kennedy knew exactly when to turn on the speed—the split second the ball was snapped. In change leadership, there is no simple, universal signal that tells us when it is the right moment to act with lightning speed.

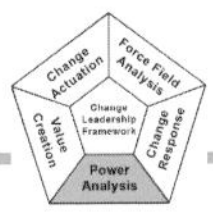




## What I Need to Do

Part of the art of change leadership is knowing when to conserve resources and credibility and when the opportune moment comes to act swiftly and implement change. When you do see a real, bona fide opportunity—when the time is clearly right—don't hesitate; act with lightning speed. Then, you will be like Kennedy standing over the quarterback celebrating a sack. Except, you will be cashing your commission check.

Be mindful, though, that speed can also require more power and may even increase tension. Remember how power is force times speed? The faster the force is exerted, the more power it involves. If the "natural" pace of a change implementation is over six months and you try to make it happen in three months, you will certainly have to work twice as hard, if not harder.

The key is to adapt to the "natural" course of events in each situation. By "natural" I mean the sequence and timing of events that consume the least amount of resources; similar to how Sun Tzu says water finds a "natural course" of least resistance.



## Action Summary

- Adapt quickly and act quickly.
- Look for the "natural course."
- Avoid tension with swift action, but be careful not to cause tension in the process.

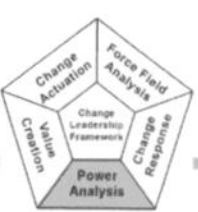


# SECRET # 62
# CALCULATE THE FORMULA FOR CHANGE

*Some men see things as they are and say why.*
*I dream things that never were and say why not?*
*—George Bernard Shaw*

## WHAT I NEED TO KNOW

"The Formula for Change," developed by Richard Beckhard and David Gleicher, is a useful tool for assessing the situation and determining next steps in your sales cycle. The fundamental premise of the formula is that driving forces must exceed resisting forces:

$$D * V * F > E + P$$

Where,

**D = Dissatisfaction**. Dissatisfaction with the current situation.

**V = Vision**. A clear vision of the positive outcome that a change could bring.

**F = First steps**. A clear understanding of the first steps that can be taken toward executing the change.

**E = Economic**. Economic costs including labor, materials, and so on.

**P = Psychological**. Emotional and other psychological costs such as stress, culture change, and so on.

Notice that the driving factors are multiplicative, meaning all of the driving factors must be present in order for the change to happen. The resisting factors are additive because the presence of either will hinder change.

## What I Need to Do

The Formula for Change provides straightforward, prescriptive guidance:

- Reinforce dissatisfaction with the status quo
- Clarify and reinforce the benefits of the change
- Identify and clarify the specific, concrete steps that will be taken to initiate the change
- Minimize the effort, cost, and risk of making the change
- Minimize psychological and emotional factors that hinder change

Using the formula to calculate the relative magnitude of driving and resisting forces is much trickier. For example, how do you measure the magnitude of dissatisfaction relative to the economic costs? You basically have two options: (1) describe all the factors in economic terms (e.g., opportunity costs become a proxy for dissatisfaction) or (2) measure all of the factors on a weighted scale. You have probably already developed an economic justification for the change, so the formula is useful as a guide for leading it.



## Action Summary

- Use the factors of D, V, and F to qualify new prospects.
- Systematically follow the guidance of the formula.
- Develop a standardized scale across your sales team.

# SECRET # 63
# CALCULATE THE FORCE FOR CHANGE

*The most rewarding things you do in life are often the ones that look like they cannot be done.*

*—Arnold Palmer*

## WHAT I NEED TO KNOW

I first described the "Force for Change" model in *Forceful Selling*—you can think of it as the "force" in *Forceful Selling*.

$$Force\ for\ Change = C * U * S - SC$$

**C =** **Criticality**. How critical is the situation for the person or organization? Is the current situation just an inconvenience? Or at the other extreme, is it life-threatening?

**U =** **Urgency**. How urgent is the situation? Is there a specific event or force that will compel the person or organization to take action at a specific time?

**S =** **Confidence**. How confident is the person in the likelihood of success of the proposed change?

**SC =** **Switching costs**. What are the costs of implementing a new situation or solution, plus the costs of disposing the current solution, plus the emotional and psychological costs associated with switching to the new solution?

Rather than weighing the forces on each side of the fulcrum, the Force for Change formula measures the degree to which the driving forces exceed the switching costs, similar to traditional return-on-investment calculations used in capital budgeting.

## What I Need to Do

First, use the Force for Change formula to qualify prospective customers and change opportunities. If the associated criticality, urgency, and confidence are all low, you will have low success finding support for the change. Likewise, if the status quo is firmly implanted (e.g., all 100,000 of the customer's employees have learned to use your competitor's product), dislodging the status quo will be difficult. Your resources may be better utilized in other accounts.

Second, look for opportunities and develop products and services that address highly critical and urgent business issues in your target market. Try to avoid "nice to have" products and find ways to make them more critical and urgent. If, after exhausting all ideas and hope, your product is still a nice-to-have, you need to assess your personal Formula for Change and Force for Change calculations and consider selling a different product.

Last, but certainly not least, use the Force for Change factors to guide your tactics, for example, raise confidence or lower switching costs.



## Action Summary

- Use C, U, and S to qualify prospective opportunities.
- Look for high C, U, and S opportunities.
- Always try to lower switching costs.

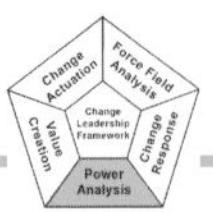


# SECRET # 64
# DETERMINE PIVOTS, MULTIPLIERS, AND TRIGGERS

*Life is always at some turning point.*

*—Irwin Edman*

## WHAT I NEED TO KNOW

### Pivots

In physics, the pivot point is the location around which a force is applied and motion occurs. In change leadership, the pivotal issue is the central issue that determines the direction of change.

### Multipliers

In physics, leverage is related to the distance from the pivot point to the place where the force is applied. By moving farther from the pivot point, the same amount of force is essentially multiplied.

Pivots and leverage are closely related because you can change the effective force by either moving the pivot point, or the place where the force is applied. In either case, a small force has disproportionately large effects.

### Triggers

Triggers are the ultimate in disproportionate results. Imagine an ancient medieval catapult with hundreds of pounds of rocks loaded in its basket. And imagine all the power required to pull the catapult down into its "loaded" position. Only a small stick holds the hundreds of pounds of force in place. It takes just the tiniest force to dislodge the stick and unleash all the power stored in the catapult.

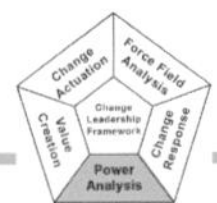




## WHAT I NEED TO DO

When you are driving change, a bewildering number of forces are at play. Sometimes it seems there are so many conflicting views, goals, and ideas that you will not get stakeholders to agree on the color of the sky, much less agree on making a significant change. There is an antidote for the chaos, though—look for the pivot points and force multipliers. The key is to find that one pivotal point, or that one lever, that will multiply the forces and tip the scale toward action.

It is said that wealth requires leverage, where one unit of effort produces multiple units of output. Be a wealthy change leader by using force multipliers to leverage change successfully.

Often people and organizations are "fully loaded," or as Lewin would call it, "in high tension," with massive forces precariously held in place. The smallest event can trigger the release of all that tension, all those forces. Look for triggers and utilize them as tools for change. But also be careful not to step unwittingly on a trigger—and blow up a land mine in your face.



## ACTION SUMMARY

- Look for the people, forces, and events that have disproportionate influence.
- Drive people toward the pivotal issues and away from smaller distractions.
- Identify events that will compel action.

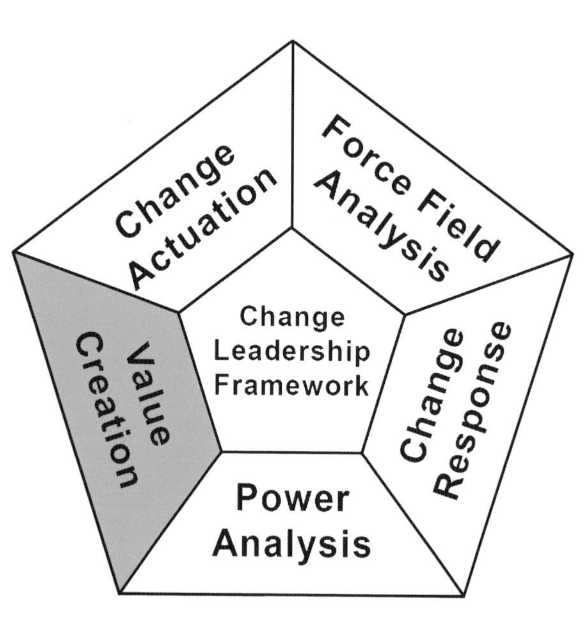
Change Actuation
Force Field Analysis
Change Leadership Framework
Value Creation
Change Response
Power Analysis

# VALUE CREATION

## THE FOURTH DISCIPLINE

# INTRODUCTION

TO

# VALUE CREATION

### What is it?

Value creation is the process of mining the customer's organization or life for sources of value.

It is important to note that the value creation discipline could be performed before the power analysis discipline, or even before change response analysis. Over the course of an ongoing account relationship, many aspects of the five disciplines may occur in parallel. In many cases, though, a coalition may have already formed around a specific change proposal and the question then becomes how to obtain approval for the change. The value creation discipline then becomes a critical step that must be completed before the change can be initiated.

### Why is it important?

Value creation is essential because people must clearly understand the value and benefits of changing before they will act to make the change. Also, your income is directly proportional to the value you create for your customers.

### How is it new or different?

The traditional approach is to prospect a sales territory for customers who have problems solved by your product. The process is like panning for gold by looking under every rock and clump of sand.

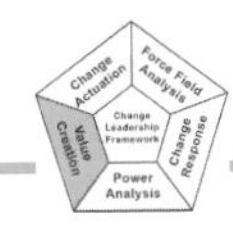


The change-centric approach is to focus on a key set of customers and mine their organization or life for opportunities to change. Then, rather than seeking to solve a problem, the salesperson seeks also to help customers achieve their goals. The process is like excavating a mine shaft deep into an organization and discovering the mother-lode of value.

## What are the common misconceptions?

The traditional approach to selling value is to define the return on investment (ROI) associated with solving a problem. But, in today's globalized, Internet-empowered world, defining ROI, which I refer to as business value, is necessary but not sufficient to build profitable differentiation. To consistently win deals at attractive margins, change-centric salespeople add far more value by proactively finding opportunities to help customers achieve their goals.

## What are the key take-aways & how do I put them in action?

Customers realize the most value not by solving problems, but by achieving their goals. Rather than asking, "What are your pains?", ask, "What are your goals?"

You will create more value for the customer and you open up far more sales opportunities for yourself.

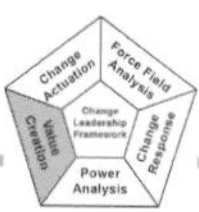


# SECRET # 65
# BE A MINER, NOT A PROSPECTOR

*The mother lode is always below the surface.*
*—Brett Clay*

## WHAT I NEED TO KNOW

Many of the concepts in the Change Leadership Framework are broadly applicable, whether you are driving large-scale change in enterprise infrastructure or driving smaller-scale change as a residential real estate agent. However, *Selling Change* is not a book about cold-calling, qualifying opportunities, and managing a funnel of many customers. *Selling Change* is about maximizing the business opportunity one account at a time. Does that mean prospecting is not necessary or important? Prospecting is certainly a critical component of success in transactional and solution-oriented sales environments. But high-value change leadership requires an entirely different approach—mining for gold.

Your client's organization is the mountain where the gold mine is located. Or, in an individual consumer context, the mountain is the person's life. All the rocks and soil in the mountain are the company's operations. The veins of gold that run through the mountain are sources of value. What is the value, then?

Abraham Maslow would say value is created when a need is satisfied. Kurt Lewin would say value is created when a person reaches a goal in her life space. In the Change Leadership Framework, I define value as the measure of the benefit realized by achieving a change.

## WHAT I NEED TO DO

The fundamental premise of change-centric selling is that value is created by change. Your role, then, is to mine the customer's organization or life for opportunities to change.

Contrast this with (1) transactional selling, where value is created by providing the best price and delivery terms and the salesperson's role is to drive awareness of availability and (2) solution-oriented selling, where value is created by solving problems and the salesperson's role is to search for problems solved by his product.

Because the only constant in life is change, change-centric selling provides a constant flow of opportunities in an account. Your job is to create those opportunities and deliver change.

Because you are delivering change, rather than products, you may find you have to detach yourself, or even divorce yourself, from your products. Notice that in doing so, you also become customer-centric and customer dependent, rather than product- or problem-centric. So, choose your customers wisely.

## ACTION SUMMARY

- Look for opportunities in your account, rather than accounts with opportunities.
- Create value by creating change.
- Sell change, rather than products.

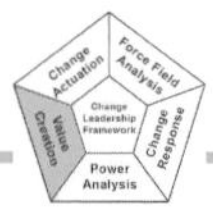


# SECRET # 66
# CREATE ORGANIZATIONAL VALUE

*The value of an idea lies in the using of it.*

*—Thomas Edison*

## WHAT I NEED TO KNOW

I previously defined value as the measure of the benefit realized by achieving a change. What does this mean, specifically, in an organizational context?

As we learn in business school and hear about every day in reports from stock markets, the purpose of a company is to create shareholder wealth. If there were a "Business School 101" course, it would teach us that shareholder wealth is created by creating profits and that profits are created by maximizing revenues and minimizing costs. So ultimately, sources of value in a profit-seeking organization are changes that increase revenue or reduce cost.

Nonprofit and public-sector organizations are a little different than companies that exist to create shareholder wealth. These organizations exist to carry out a mission that ultimately creates utility for their constituents. For example, I had a client with the mission of improving the security of information technology across the Internet. To carry out such missions, nonprofit and public-sector organizations must fund their activities by collecting revenue and minimizing costs. So sources of value for these organizations also include changes that increase revenue and reduce cost, but also include an additional source—accomplishing the mission of the organization.

## What I Need to Do

Aaah...if it were only that easy to increase revenue, decrease cost, and solve world hunger.

While changes ultimately achieve these goals, an organization may benefit in many ways from making changes. Here is a partial list that quickly comes to mind:

- Improved competitiveness
- Reduced market risk
- Improved employee morale
- Improved customer satisfaction
- Improved regulatory compliance
- Improved balance sheet
- Improved agility

Any change that helps the organization respond to the Four Forces acting on it creates value for it. You will need, however, to put the value in the organization's lexicon for the value to be recognized.

## Action Summary

- Create value by improving revenue, cost, and mission.
- Identify any and all other benefits.
- Translate value into the language and perspective of the customer.

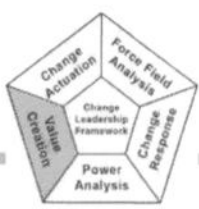


# SECRET # 67
# CREATE PERSONAL VALUE

*Classic economic theory...could be revolutionized by accepting the reality of higher human needs, including the impulse to self-actualization and the love for the highest values.*

*—Abraham Maslow*

## WHAT I NEED TO KNOW

An important point often overlooked is that people participate in organizations for one ultimate purpose—to derive personal value.

Demonstrating measurable business results related to a change in the organization's culture, strategies, or environmental factors has very high value. But to create maximum value, a change must satisfy the internal needs of the organization—the "self." I call that "self-aligned value."

But, not only must the internal need(s) of the organization be satisfied, but the internal needs of the individuals in the organization must also be satisfied. People participate in the organization to satisfy their Maslowian needs, whether they are basic needs for food and shelter, or higher needs for safety, belonging, or esteem. The higher the type of need being satisfied, the higher the value created.

So in addition to creating value for the organization, the change leader must create personal value for the members.

## What I Need to Do

When mining for value, also look for sources of personal value for people in the organization. Examples include:

**Maslowian needs—self-aligned value**. Anything that increases income, increases safety, reduces risk, enhances belonging, or improves esteem for the individual will be a source of personal value.

**The Four Forces**. Anything that helps people improve their positions in one of the four force dimensions will create personal value.

**Political goals**. One way or the other, all people have political goals and strategies. When the change leader helps the individual achieve these political goals, far more value is created than what appears in a financial justification.

**Opportunities and comfort**. Any change that provides either an opportunity for the person to enhance her position in some fashion or a way to increase her comfort creates personal value.

## Action Summary

- Mine for personal value, as well as organizational value.
- Strive to deliver the highest value: self-aligned value.
- Be creative—even improving personal comfort can be highly valued.

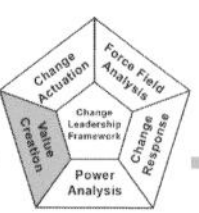


# SECRET # 68
# CREATE STRATEGIC VALUE

*Strive not to be a success, but rather to be of value.*
*—Albert Einstein*

## WHAT I NEED TO KNOW

How do you know if you are creating strategic value? Here are some things to look for:

**Force fan out**. How far do the forces of change fan out through the organization?

**Quantitative evidence**. To what degree can the forces of change be quantified and verified?

**Impact on financials**. Cash is still king—even in change leadership. The quantifiable evidence must ultimately increase shareholder wealth through increased revenues, lower costs, and lower risks.

**Impact on critical success factors**. Every organization has a handful of factors upon which its success hinges. How much do those factors depend on the change?

**Duration of impact**. The longer the impact, the more strategic the value.

**Self-aligned value**. The ultimate strategic value is derived by satisfying both the organization's internal needs as well as the internal needs of the highest executives.

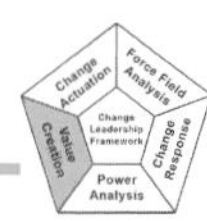



## What I Need to Do

Be creative and build a checklist of all the ways you could possibly create strategic value for the customer. Use the list on the previous page to stimulate your thinking. Then, build as much value into your change proposal as possible.

Also, refer to Michael Porter's Five Forces model for additional strategic value metrics:

- Does the proposed change help the client differentiate the organization and its products and services?
- Does the proposed change reduce the intensity of the competitive rivalry (within the limits of the law)?
- Are you helping the client increase barriers for new companies to enter into its market?
- Does the change increase the bargaining power of the organization with its suppliers?
- Does the change increase the bargaining power of the organization with its customers?



## Action Summary

- Maximize your value by creating strategic value for the customer.
- Try to quantify and verify the value whenever possible.
- Make sure the customer takes ownership for realizing the value, or she won't recognize it.

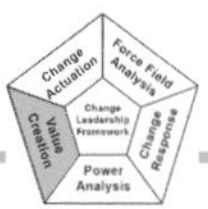


# SECRET # 69
# CLIMB THE VALUE HIERARCHY

*Create the highest, grandest vision possible for your life because you become what you believe.*

*—Oprah Winfrey*

## WHAT I NEED TO KNOW

The drawing on the opposite page illustrates the concept of the Value Hierarchy and how value grows larger at the top.

**Features**. Countless salespeople, marketers, and executives confuse features with benefits. Features simply describe a product—they do not have value.

**Benefits**. When a feature is used to accomplish something for the buyer, it generates a benefit.

**Solutions**. When a benefit solves a problem for the buyer, it starts to have measurable value.

**Qualitative results**. The solution to a problem should result in some positive outcomes (e.g., improved quality, improved profitability).

**Quantitative results**. When the results can be measured and verified, they will be perceived at their full amount and can be objectively plugged into the company's financial statements to assess their impact.

**Change response**. When the product or service helps the customer respond to forces that threaten opportunities, the value is more significant than numbers alone would suggest.

**Self-aligned**. The greatest value is derived when the customer satisfies his most cherished internal needs.

## What I Need to Do

Climb the value hierarchy as quickly as you can.

If the nature of your product involves a mostly transactional sales process and your customers are only interested in features, refer those customers to your website shopping cart. Become the best Internet marketer possible and stay current with the fast-changing technologies and techniques of the Internet.

If you are currently focused on delivering solutions, your business proposals should already identify quantifiable results. Climb the Value Hierarchy by identifying high-impact forces acting on the customer and internal needs that can be satisfied with your solution.

To achieve and maintain a position at the top of the Value Hierarchy, be creative and agile with your "solution." You will almost certainly have to adapt your solution to deliver value at that level.

## Action Summary

- Transact features, benefits, and solutions on your website.
- Identify qualitative and quantitative results early in the sales cycle.
- As your relationship forms, identify the most important forces and the most cherished needs, and then deliver on them.

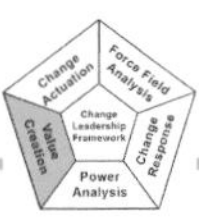


# SECRET # 70
# THE CUSTOMER OWNS THE MINE

*There are risks and costs to a program of action, but they are far less than the long-range risks and costs of comfortable inaction.*

*—John F. Kennedy*

## WHAT I NEED TO KNOW

You can do great things for people, but if they do not appreciate them, what have you accomplished? More important, if you have created huge value for your customer, but he does not recognize or appreciate it, your compensation will be commensurate with the value your customer perceives, not the value you created.

When we are in the role of helping people, sometimes we want so much to help them that we take ownership for their situation ourselves. If you have parents or children, you know how frustrating it can be when they fail to follow your well-informed suggestion. It's like leading a horse to water. You feel like saying, "If you don't drink the water in the trough, you're going to die. Look, if you don't drink it, I'm going to drink it for you!"

Just as in our roles as parents or children we cannot drink the water for the people we are trying to help, as salespeople and change leaders, we cannot make the change for our customers.

From time to time, when we are deeply involved with an account—we are deep in the proverbial mine shaft, if you will—it consumes our life and we forget who owns the mine. Ultimately, the mountain you are mining is owned by the customer.

The value you find in the mine is the value the customer perceives, not the value you perceive. Also, it is the customer who creates the value. You are merely the customer's helper.

## What I Need to Do

Go ahead and be passionate. Go ahead and passionately care about helping your customers. If you do not sincerely derive satisfaction from helping your customers, you will not be a successful change-centric salesperson.

Go ahead and imagine yourself in the customer's shoes. Imagine the forces the customer is feeling and how the customer can best respond to them.

But, stop short of believing you are actually living in the customer's shoes. Stop short of believing the shoes are yours.

Experienced teachers set clear boundaries for their ownership because they know some "horses" will drink from the trough and some will not, regardless of the teacher's actions and best intentions. Set similar boundaries for your ownership.

Make sure the customer personally takes ownership, every step along the way, for the value you help create.



## Action Summary

- Help people only as much as they want to be helped.
- Don't take ownership for the customer's change response.
- Make sure the customer takes ownership for the value—from the very beginning to the very end.

# SECRET # 71
# CHANGE THE RULES

*The time to win a fight is before it starts.*
*—Frederick W. Lewis*

## WHAT I NEED TO KNOW

Economists use a term called BATNA, which stands for the "best alternative to a negotiated agreement." The notion is that if the customer has a better alternative he is going to take the alternative. So your proposal has to be at least as attractive as the customer's next best option. How is BATNA related to mining for value? It determines how much of the gold you get to keep.

You can make your proposal more attractive than the BATNA by changing the rules of the competition.

**Traditional Rules**

- Who has the best price?
- Who has the best solution?
- Who has the most benefits?
- Who generates the most business results?

**Change Leadership Rules**

- Who can best help the client respond to the forces of change?
- Who can best help the client reach a new destination in her life space?
- Who can create the most self-aligned value for the client?

Playing the change leadership game enables you to become a strategic resource for which your client will find few alternatives.

## What I Need to Do

First, make sure you are following all of Sun Tzu's guidance for engaging opponents. For example, Sun Tzu says, if you and your competitor are equally strong and play by the same rules, you will win some of the time. Increase your wins and your revenues by playing to your competitor's flank (i.e., areas of weakness, whether lack of focus, resources, skill, etc.).

Second, work with the customer to identify, quantify, and verify the business results generated by your proposed change.

Then, eliminate your competition by changing the rules and delivering more value.

Be "at the top of your game" by playing at the top of the Value Hierarchy and delivering strategic and self-aligned value.

Lock out your competitor by consistently delivering high value and increasing your customer's dependence on you as a strategic resource.

## Action Summary

- Understand the rules your competitors are playing by—then, play by different rules.
- Deliver verifiable business results, but don't stop there.
- Deliver strategic and self-aligned value.

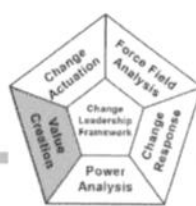


# SECRET # 72
# MAINTAIN HIGH VALUE

*The most interesting thing about a postage stamp is the persistence with which it sticks to its job.*

*—Napoleon Hill*

## WHAT I NEED TO KNOW

Establish high value and stick to it. Do not deliver high value and then discount its price.

Establishing high value requires a tremendous amount of discipline and self-control—primarily the discipline not to take shortcuts. If you do not have that level of discipline, it is unlikely you will have created high value to begin with. But once you have gone to all the effort to create high value, the last thing you want to do is throw it all away by reducing the price.

When you have successfully helped the customer make an important change, then he will be sincerely grateful. He will feel indebted to you beyond the money that exchanges hands.

It is not only fair for you to share in the value you create, your survival depends on it. The decision to pursue the strategy of creating and obtaining high value is irrevocable because creating high value requires a completely different set of business practices and a much higher cost structure than, say, transactional selling at the other end of the spectrum.

Rather than trying to speed along an order with a price reduction, what about taking the opposite approach? You could say, "These changes are significant and will take time to execute correctly. If you want to accelerate them, it will increase the cost. But the sooner the changes are initiated, the more we'll be able to manage those costs. Would you like to go ahead and get started today?"

## WHAT I NEED TO DO

If the customer's organization employs professional purchasing agents who are paid to reduce your price, rather than maximize their company's value, do the following:

- Do not expend any of your company's resources until you have a firm contract in place. You do not want to be at the mercy of a purchasing agent after you have delivered all the value and exhausted your resources.
- Confidently tell the customer you are in the business of creating value—and that you stay in business by sharing in the value you create.
- Ask your grateful customer to intervene on your behalf. Remind your customer of all you are doing for her.
- Build a solid, irrefutable case for the value you are delivering and do not back down from it.

Creating high value requires maintaining high value, starting long before your first customer meeting. Continually ask yourself, "Is the task I am performing right now maintaining high value?"



## ACTION SUMMARY

- Every action you perform should be high quality and be geared toward generating high value.
- Align your cost structure with the value you can create—and share—with the customer.
- Document the value you create and make sure your customer verifies it and "owns" it.

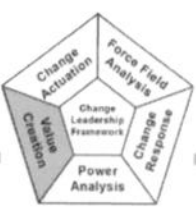


# Secret # 73
# Be Outstanding

*The quality of a person's life is in direct proportion to their commitment to excellence . . .*

*—Vince Lombardi*

## What I Need to Know

Many years ago, I took my sales team to a Tony Robbins motivational seminar. One of Robbins' biggest points was the power of being outstanding. He cited example after example of how the person in first place gets almost all of the rewards and recognition. The other finishers may only be behind by milliseconds, but they essentially get no recognition.

During the 2008 Summer Olympics, what athlete gained the most recognition? Swimmer Michael Phelps. He earned recognition because he placed first in eight different races. He won one of the races by one one-hundreth of a second! In an interview after the race, Phelps said that when he watched the slow-motion video of his and the other swimmer's hands touching the wall, he could not see whose hand touched first. Do you know the name of the other swimmer? Likely not. Yet, he swam just as fast as Phelps.

Here is one more of a limitless number of examples. Tour de France cyclists race for many hours over thousands of miles over three weeks. The winner is usually no more than ten minutes faster than the tenth place finisher. I remember one year, 2003, when the winner finished just one minute ahead of second place—after racing for 5,021 minutes! I will bet you only recognize the name of the winner, Lance Armstrong, and do not recognize the name of Jan Ullrich—even though they essentially finished at the same time. Lance Armstrong is called one of the best athletes of all time. What is Jan Ullrich called?

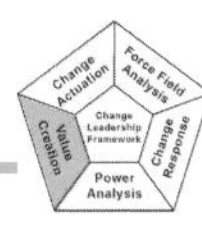




## What I Need to Do

To be an outstanding salesperson, deliver outstanding results for your customer. You will then enjoy the "halo effect"—people giving you more credit than you deserve. Opportunities will come your way faster than you can deliver them.

Just do not make the mistake of sacrificing your outstanding delivery to take on more opportunities than you can handle.

You will definitely stand out in your customer's mind if you help the customer make the changes that respond to the customer's most pressing forces and achieve the customer's most cherished internal needs.

You will also be outstanding, at least by definition, if you play by different rules than your competitors. Make your rules consistency, trust, and high value.



## Action Summary

- Identify ways you can deliver outstanding value to your customer.
- Ask your customer how you can be outstanding.
- Be change-centric and deliver self-aligned value.

# SECRET # 74
# FOCUS ON YOURSELF

*One's only rival is one's own potentialities. One's only failure is failing to live up to one's own possibilities.*
*—Abraham Maslow*

## WHAT I NEED TO KNOW

In *The Art of War,* Sun Tzu wrote:

> If you know the enemy and know yourself, you need not fear the result of a hundred battles. If you know yourself but not the enemy, for every victory gained you will also suffer a defeat. If you know neither the enemy nor yourself, you will succumb in every battle.

Sun Tzu certainly offers good advice to be heeded. But change leadership is different from war in a very fundamental way—there is no enemy. If you are selling solutions, there are many competitive solutions or "enemies." But if you are a change agent, the only enemies are your own anxieties. Let's reformulate Sun Tzu's famous words for change leadership:

> If you focus on being the best change agent you can be, you need not fear the result of a hundred battles. If you focus on being a better change agent than the competitor, for every victory gained you will also suffer a defeat. If you focus not on being a change agent, but rather on providing the best solution, you will succumb in every battle.

Being an elite change leader is similar to being an elite athlete. Do people like Lance Armstrong, Tiger Woods, and Michael Phelps set their sights on other people? No, they do not. They are in front—there is no one to follow.

## What I Need to Do

Is Tiger Woods the best golfer because all the other golfers are worse than he is? Or is Tiger Woods a great golfer—period? What makes him great? Think about this: Tiger Woods is not great. Tiger Woods' flawless execution is great.

How does Tiger achieve his flawless execution? Does he walk from hole to hole hoping his competitors' balls miss the cup? Absolutely not. Tiger wins by making sure his ball goes in the cup. He makes his balls go in the cup by completely focusing on his own execution. He plays every stroke as if it were the game-deciding stroke.

Would you like to be the Tiger Woods of your business? Would you like to be an outstanding achiever at the top of your game? Would you like your customers to chase you with orders instead of you chasing them? This can all happen if you focus on being the best change leader you can be. It is an endless journey of discovery and learning. But it is an incredibly rewarding journey.

## Action Summary

- Focus on your own execution, not the competition's execution.
- Reduce your anxieties by increasing your preparation.
- "Play" every element of your game as if it meant the difference between winning and losing.

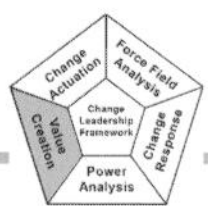


# Secret # 75
# Be Willing to Walk

*Actions speak louder than words.*
*—Theodore Roosevelt*

## What I Need to Know

One of the tenets of negotiation theory is that a deal will not close until both parties overcome the reluctance to walk away from the deal. So as counterintuitive as it may seem, you have to be willing to walk before you can get the order.

As I look back over my own career, I realize I may have been overly ambitious and impatient at times. There may have been some instances where I could have gained more by taking the deal than walking away. But there were also times where I should have walked away and didn't. Ultimately though, I believe people usually err more on the side of setting their goals too low, selling themselves short, and accepting mediocre outcomes more often than they err on the side of walking away from gift horses.

Walking away from a potential opportunity is a hard decision. So, how do you know when to do it?

First, determine how much value you want to deliver and make the necessary investments.

Next, set criteria and goals for yourself and measure potential clients and changes against those criteria. If you want to be a highly valued change leader, you cannot tie up your resources with low-value changes. So you must be willing to walk away if your criteria are not met. It's definitely scary. But remember: The deal will not close until you are prepared to walk.

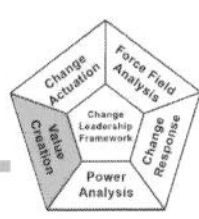



## What I Need to Do

The first thing to do is not to be a fool. The economic discipline of game theory has a concept called "reservation price." Reservation price is the price at which you are *truly* indifferent to whether you get the deal or not. Both buyers and sellers do themselves a tremendous disservice when they (a) fool themselves with inaccurate or emotional assessments of their reservation price, and (b) negotiate using a number that is different from their real reservation price. For example, if you say, "$100 is my best price" when you really would have accepted $80, you would lose an opportunity if the customer would have accepted $90.

Be disciplined in (a) thoroughly and objectively assessing your reservation price and other criteria, (b) walking away from opportunities that do not meet your price or criteria, and (c) quoting your real reservation price, even when there is a risk of "leaving money on the table."



## Action Summary

- Determine your overall strategy and goals.
- After much soul searching and objective analysis, determine your reservation price.
- Remember, *both* parties must be willing to walk before they are willing to close.

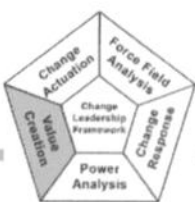

# SECRET # 76
# DON'T BEG—DELIVER

*You can't build a reputation on what you are going to do.*
*—Henry Ford*

## WHAT I NEED TO KNOW

Be honest. Have you been at the end of a quarter needing to make your number and felt a strong urge to beg your customer for an order?

Have you been reading the secrets of value creation in this book and caught yourself thinking, "This author is whacko...Creating high value is too much work...My grandchildren will be inheriting the orders in my pipeline if I do all of that...I'm just going to close the order for whatever I can get and move on to the next one...Why do I care about high value, anyway?!"

The answer to both questions is: If you don't deliver high value, you won't get the order. Period.

Remember, whether it happens tomorrow, or next year, or the year after, your competition is going to be just a mouse click away for the customer. If you do not deliver high value, someone else will.

The way to build a solid, predictable order pipeline is to deliver high value. You will always have high value if you deliver change. Once you are aligned with the customer's needs for change, the customer will be pushing you to deliver instead of you pushing him for the order. You will have a bookings backlog instead of a bookings pipeline.

## What I Need to Do

Rather than using "push" tactics and thinking how to accelerate orders, you may get better results by using "pull" tactics and thinking how you can deliver more value.

I'm sure you have heard the expression, "You get what you pay for." Set customers' expectations for paying a fair price for what they receive.

Have you heard the expression, "You get what you deliver"? When you deliver high value, you get high revenue and profits. When you deliver low value, you get low revenue and profits.

Make your decision and then live by it: Do you want to be a beggar? Or do you want to be a change leader? While this may seem like an overdramatization and while both options involve certain hardships, these stark terms appropriately reflect undeniable trends: globalization of competition, Internet empowerment, and the most difficult and complicated economic environment since the Great Depression.

## Action Summary

- Focus on high-value delivery.
- Let others beg for low value deals.
- Meet and exceed reciprocal expectations of fairness.

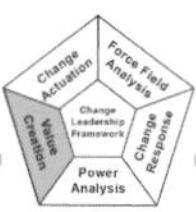


# Secret # 77
# There Are No Secrets

*If you do build a great experience, customers tell each other about that. Word of mouth is very powerful.*

*—Jeff Bezos*

## What I Need to Know

George Orwell's classic novel *Nineteen Eighty-Four* depicted what is becoming a truly terrifying reality of the twenty-first century. Orwell envisioned a world where people had access to every bit of information about you—even your thoughts. A famous scene is a bedroom where a plaque above the bed is actually a "telescreen" that allows full visibility into the main character's life. Because Winston Smith's thoughts wander to things that are not politically correct, the Thought Police torture Winston with his fear of rats. With every passing day, that scene becomes less fiction and more reality.

In the Internet-empowered world of the twenty-first century, you cannot hide. If you deliver bad quality to a particular client, all six billion people on the planet will know about it. Or at least they can know about it with a couple clicks on the computer.

This presents both opportunities and risks. The opportunity is to deliver outstanding value and then become overwhelmed with business opportunities. The risks are that the tiniest dissatisfied customer could tarnish your reputation or your competitors could sabotage you by putting misleading information on the Internet.

There is not a lot you can personally do about unethical behavior on the Internet. But you can make sure you conduct yourself with the utmost integrity and outstanding quality. If you don't, everyone on the planet will surely know all about it.

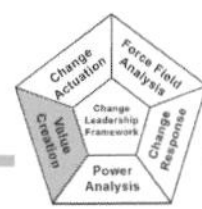



## What I Need to Do

One approach that seems almost inevitable is to satisfy customers—at all costs. But this can quickly become unprofitable.

A better approach is to choose customers wisely, then satisfy them fully. In other words, have closer relationships with fewer customers. Wise customer choices include customers who:

- Are rational, fair, and trustworthy
- See you as a strategic resource
- Derive the most economic value from your relationship
- Ultimately generate the most profits for you over the lifetime of your relationship

All other customers simply lower your profit margins. Of course, the choice between revenue and margins is an age-old dilemma for executives and scholars alike. The collapse of many companies in the late 2000s will provide fodder for a whole new generation to study this question. However, the change leader's decision is simple: It is better to be small and successful, than large and tenuous.

## Action Summary

- Zealously maintain your brand.
- Have closer relationships with fewer customers.
- Disengage from marginally profitable customer relationships.

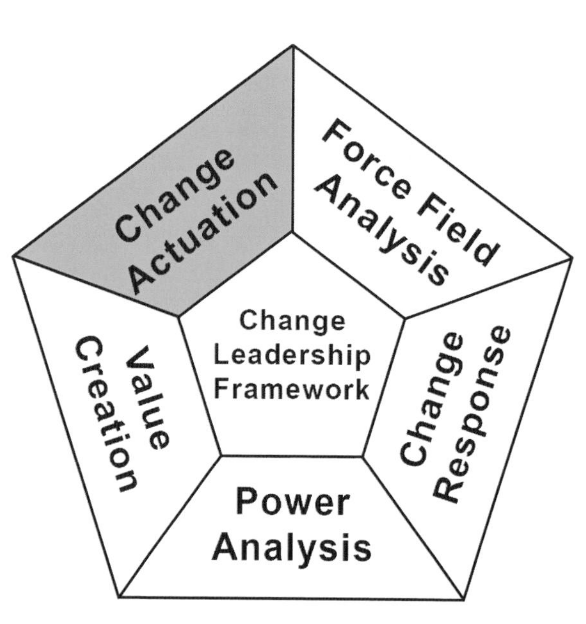
Change Actuation
Force Field Analysis
Change Leadership Framework
Value Creation
Change Response
Power Analysis

# CHANGE ACTUATION

## THE FIFTH DISCIPLINE

# INTRODUCTION

## TO

# CHANGE ACTUATION

---

### What is it?

Change actuation is the process of putting the change in motion.

### Why is it important?

All the effort and investment involved in the first four disciplines only counts if you make the change happen. This is where your success or failure is measured.

### How is it new or different?

One of the guiding principles of the Change Leadership Framework is that the most difficult step in executing change is the first. Therefore, the fifth discipline of the Change Leadership Framework is "change actuation" (rather than "change execution").

*Webster's Dictionary* defines "actuate" as:

1. To put into action or motion; to move or incite to action; to influence actively; to move as motives do

The same Latin root, *actus,* is found in the word "actualize," which *Webster's* defines as:

1. To make actual; to realize in action

Does the word "actualize" sound familiar? Remember that the highest need at the top of Maslow's hierarchy of needs is "self-actualization."

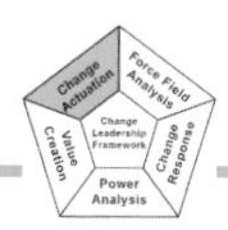




The Change Leadership Framework comes full circle. It starts with force field analysis and understanding the person's internal needs, ranging from physiological to self-actualization. And it ends with actuating the changes that will help the person satisfy those needs.

### What are the common misconceptions?

You might expect a book on change leadership to be all about the process of executing change—in essence "cracking the whip over the horse's head and steering the wagon." Execution is absolutely critical. After all, what good is a map if you never arrive at the destination? Furthermore, after reading this far in the book, you probably have the word "delivery" indelibly imprinted on your corneas.

So, how do you excel in the execution and delivery of change? The bottom line is: That question is out of the scope of the Change Leadership Framework. In an organizational context, change execution is treated in areas of study such as "project and program management," "change management," and "organizational development." In an individual context, it is treated in areas of study such as "human psychology" and "self-improvement." Many useful tools are provided by those areas of study and the Change Leadership Framework utilizes important concepts and tools from them.

However, "change leadership" is very different from "change management." Leadership is about things like direction, motivation, initiation, and achievement. Management is about things like organizing, monitoring, correcting, and completing. The focus of this book is on leadership, not management.



### What are the key take-aways & how do I put them in action?

Delivering and executing high-value change are absolutely critical. However, if you focus primarily on the motivations, direction, initiation and achievements associated with the changes, then their execution will be much smoother.

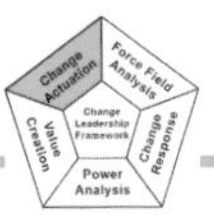


# SECRET # 78
# BE AN AGENT OF CHANGE

*Only a life in the service of others is worth living.*
*—Albert Einstein*

## WHAT I NEED TO KNOW

Being a change leader means being a change agent. Being a change agent means being a change actuator. Sound confusing? Let's sort it out.

When a person demonstrates the vision, trust, and competence to lead people where they want to go—she becomes a change leader.

When people choose to follow, they entrust the leader with the authority and power to act on their behalf and to take them somewhere—they employ the leader as their agent.

Once the path is plotted and the authority granted, the change agent must then put the followers in motion—she helps actuate the change.

Regardless of the nature of your business, whether you are selling cars, airplanes, software, mutual funds, or life insurance, consider your company a "change agency." You are selling change. Think of yourself as a change agent employed not by your company, but by your client to actuate change on your client's behalf. Your company's resources, as well as those of the client are the vehicles for actuating the change.

Important tasks of the change agent include:

- Identifying value-creating opportunities
- Assembling and energizing the change team
- Brokering agreement among resource owners, including your company's resources

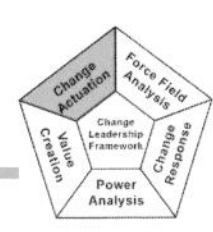




## WHAT I NEED TO DO

Climbing the value ladder and becoming a change agent that is viewed by the customer as a strategic asset is not a process that happens over night. The best way to get started is to understand everything you can about the forces affecting the customer. Then, help the customer respond to the biggest forces. You will soon be seen as a "friend of the company."

The next step is to understand the customer's organization and characterize the people in it. You want to understand what drives them and how they behave. The Four Forces model is very useful for this.

Based on your deep knowledge of the organization, you will be able to assemble change teams and build coalitions for change.

Ultimately, you must work across organizational boundaries, including your company's organization to formulate a change plan and put it in action.

## ACTION SUMMARY

- You are employed by the client to create value on her behalf.
- Demonstrate your leadership: vision, trustworthiness, and competence.
- Broker agreement on a change plan.

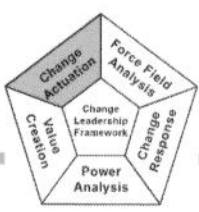


# Secret # 79
# Actuate, Rather Than Own

*If it doesn't start with you, it dies with you.*
*—Julian Casablancas*

## What I Need to Know

As the change agent, the client empowers you to put the change into motion. However, it is critical to understand the difference between actuating a change and owning it. The client, not you, owns the change.

Clients naturally want the vendor to take care of everything. That's what they're paying you for, right? The client selected you over your competition because he trusts you to deliver. Since the client is extremely busy juggling many problems, he does not have time to babysit you. So he holds you accountable.

Many years ago, when I was a student of Mike Bosworth, author of *Solution Selling*, he emphatically stressed the importance of not taking ownership of the client's problem. The reason: Clients who do not take ownership of their changes do not implement them successfully. And who gets blamed? You.

You, as the change agent, are there to assist, support, analyze, compute, advise, communicate, advocate, and so on. But you cannot make the change for the client. Making a change is like assisting someone with quitting smoking. You cannot quit smoking for the client. He must quit for himself.

This is, perhaps, the most important point of this book: Do not fall into the trap of owning your customer's problems.

You have an appropriate change agent relationship when the customer views you as a fellow colleague in a two-person boat.

## What I Need to Do

Set clear expectations upfront that you will be the client's strategic resource by helping the client create high value. But ultimately, the client, not you, owns her business.

Be careful to keep the client involved. Do not let her disappear and her communications with you "go dark."

Keep communication open by putting terms in the contract whereby (a) the internal agent and key resource owners are required to meet with your team on a regular basis, and (b) the executive sponsor or business owner is required to meet with you on a regular, albeit less frequent, basis throughout the change project.

Do not shoot yourself in the foot by overselling—painting overly rosy pictures and making promises you cannot deliver. Once you do that, the customer will "own" you. You will forever be the customer's Golden Retriever answering to her every beck and call.

## Action Summary

- Do not oversell.
- Both you and the customer should consider each other as peers and hold each other mutually accountable.
- Keep the client in the boat with you.

# SECRET # 80
# THINK BIG, EXECUTE INCREMENTALLY

*Human felicity is produced not so much by great pieces of good fortune that seldom happen, as by little advantages that occur every day.*

*—Benjamin Franklin*

## WHAT I NEED TO KNOW

People are often scared by the concept of big changes. They may immediately dismiss an idea as unachievable and miss a really great opportunity.

A classic negotiating technique that makes big things seem smaller is called "nibbling." The idea is that rather than asking for a big concession all at once, you keep returning to ask for smaller concessions. When taken together, the sum of the small items is large. As humans, we can only put one foot in front of the other, anyway. So why scare ourselves with the magnitude of the task in front of us? If a change seems like a hundred marathons of effort, just focus on the step in front of you and never stop stepping. You will achieve the change sooner than you realize.

Conversely, it is also critically important to think big. If you only think incrementally, you will miss the really big opportunities. As a change leader, you must be the visionary. You must be able to see beyond your client's limited vision. Most of us usually have extremely limited vision and we grossly underestimate what is achievable. We essentially live in boxes that we create for ourselves. One way you can become a strategic resource for your client is to help him see outside of his box.

## What I Need to Do

If you or your customer has small expectations, you will reap small rewards. All of us would like bigger rewards. But because our daily lives are necessarily incremental, it is easy to get caught up in the current challenges of the day and lose sight of how small they really are.

Rather than thinking incrementally and executing incrementally, you will reap far bigger rewards if you think big and then execute incrementally. Even humanity's biggest achievements, such as the Great Wall of China, were accomplished in small increments, one brick at a time.

As you build a vision of change for your client, be careful to test what size vision is palatable at what time. In some cases, it may be better to take a "nibbling" approach, focusing the client just on the step ahead. In other cases, the client may not have patience for small items and you could lose credibility if you do not paint big pictures with big ideas.

## Action Summary

- Think big and reap big rewards.
- For execution, think small—execution most often fails due to overlooked details.
- Appraise the customer's appetite before describing the menu.

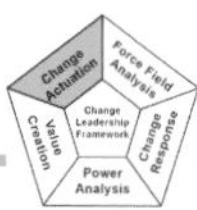


# SECRET # 81
# ALWAYS HAVE A PLAN

*To do great things, two things are necessary:*
*a plan and not quite enough time.*

*—Anonymous*

## WHAT I NEED TO KNOW

There is an old saying, "If you fail to plan, you plan to fail." In *The Art of War,* Sun Tzu says:

> Now, the general who wins a battle makes many calculations in his temple ere the battle is fought. The general who loses a battle makes but few calculations beforehand. Thus do many calculations lead to victory, and few calculations to defeat: how much more no calculation at all! It is by attention to this point that I can foresee who is likely to win or lose. (Lionel Giles translation)

Sun Tzu's words ring loud and true for change-centric selling. Do you like to plan? Do you always take the time to plan properly? Some people derive a tremendous amount of comfort and security from having developed a game plan. Others think about that task and immediately feel tired, preferring just to "wing it."

A good example of planning is professional American football. It may seem like the players rely on incredible instincts and agility to adapt to conditions on the field. But what you may not know is that before every game, football teams spend hours and hours watching "films" of the opponent to study every move the opponent makes. Then, by game day, every move the football players make has been predetermined and preprogrammed. They are simply executing the "game plan." Only after tremendous planning and preparation do the players awe us with their "amazing skill."

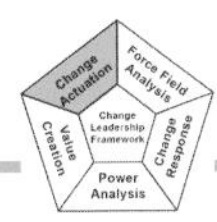



## What I Need to Do

Whether you like it or not, the reality is, the more you plan and the more you prepare, the more value you will deliver as a change agent—and the more your income will grow.

Therefore, planning skills and tools are critical if you want to grow your income. Constantly develop your skills by taking classes and staying abreast of current planning methodologies. Studies in the areas of business management and project management are also important.

Develop a standard account planning template that includes key principles of change-centric selling. Consider attending a ChangeCentric Selling® Bootcamp, which provides a rich set of account planning tools and techniques for leading change and growing revenues.

Be sure to share your account planning documents with the internal change agent in your accounts. You are partners in the same boat. So she will want to help you calibrate expectations and develop successful plans.

## Action Summary

- Plan to succeed.
- Develop planning tools that can be used repeatedly and refined over time.
- Constantly invest in your own skills.

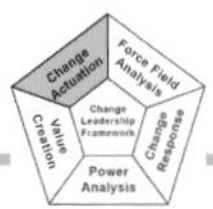


# SECRET # 82
# MEASURE TWICE; CUT ONCE

*More important than the quest for certainty*
*is the quest for clarity.*
*—Francois Gautier*

## WHAT I NEED TO KNOW

Remember the saying, "The only thing you can be sure of is death and taxes?" A change leader needs to have a healthy skepticism regarding people's views and commitments. *Webster's Dictionary* defines skepticism as:

1. An undecided, inquiring state of mind
2. The doctrine that no fact or principle can be certainly known; the tenet that all knowledge is uncertain

Healthy skepticism is understanding that everyone sees things differently. It is understanding that the data people provide is just their *view* of the data. It is understanding that two people think they are saying the same thing, but really may be talking about two entirely different things.

Carpenters have a saying, "Measure twice; cut once." Nothing is worse than the horrifying feeling of wasting several hours of effort and expensive materials with one erroneous cut. Once the cut is made, it cannot be undone. In change leadership, the equivalent of "measuring twice" is "validating twice." The equivalent of "cutting" is taking public action. If you take public action, but people disagree, then feelings, relationships, and credibility can all be damaged.

The best approach the change leader can take is to validate and revalidate stakeholder views and commitments—before acting on them.

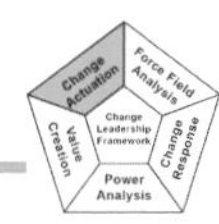




## What I Need to Do

Become knowledgeable of the host of cognitive biases that can cause stakeholders unwittingly to provide inaccurate data, (e.g., false consensus, rosy retrospection, wishful thinking, anchoring, sustainability, etc.). Then, use this knowledge to identify potentially inaccurate data.

Try to rely on verifiable facts, rather than anecdotal hearsay.

Verification of facts is the easy task. The much harder task is verifying people's views and, most important, commitments. You do not want to walk into a meeting believing you have someone's support, only to witness the person supporting the opposite view.

Build a mental dossier on each stakeholder that includes an accounting of trustworthy and untrustworthy actions you have observed from them. If they say or do things that damage other people, you have to assume they will do the same to you.

Limit your exposure to risk and your dependence on people until they have demonstrated their trustworthiness.

## Action Summary

- Have a "healthy" skepticism of people's views.
- Try to validate all data at least two ways.
- Do not be paranoid; just be sure.

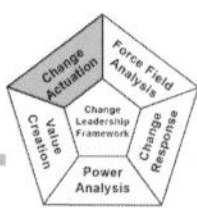


# SECRET # 83
# BIG SUCCESS = BIG RISK

*I believe that one of life's biggest risks is never daring to risk.*
*—Oprah Winfrey*

## WHAT I NEED TO KNOW

Unless you have a phobia like I have that reality television shows will irreparably kill my brain cells, then you have probably seen *The Apprentice* with Donald Trump. On the show, ambitious young workers compete for a job in Trump's empire. When competitors are eliminated, Trump points his finger at them, purses his lips, and says, "You're fired!" Donald Trump has become more than a real estate and gaming executive; he has become a bigger-than-life business mogul icon. How does he do it?

Of course, his self-esteem and self-promotion are legend. Those are definitely keys to his success. But by far the biggest key to his success has been his risk taking. Every few years, he seems to go bankrupt under billions of dollars of debt, and a few years later he is a billionaire again. This willingness to take billion-dollar risks is what makes him a billion-dollar success.

In change leadership, both the changes and their risks are borne by the client. The change agent's role is to provide objective, unbiased information to the client about the benefits and risks associated with change options. Furthermore, the change agent's role is to assist the client in eliminating and mitigating risks to ensure the change is successful.

But ultimately, the change agent has the highest value if he helps the client make the changes that produce the biggest successes.

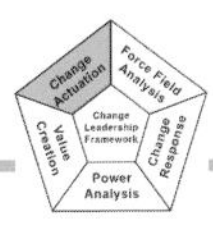


## What I Need to Do

Even though the client owns the change and the associated risk, you will be sharing in both—assuming you are an astute negotiator. So you must share similar values regarding risk tolerance and opportunity cost. For example, let's say you want to be a supplier to an auto manufacturer whose product life cycles are ten years, including three years of development. If you are not prepared to invest for three years before you begin to see revenue, you will not be able to play in that game.

Perhaps one of your biggest challenges is not convincing your client, but rather convincing your own company to take risk and play in games with bigger purses. Either way, you likely won't have much influence over their risk tolerances. Your best strategy is to become a risk management quasi expert and reduce risk as much as possible. For example, the Project Management Institute offers many great publications such as *Project Risk Management Guidelines: Managing Risk in Large Projects and Complex Procurements*, and even offers certification in risk management.

## Action Summary

- Think big—and then manage the associated risk.
- Make sure you and your client similarly value risk and opportunity costs.
- Make risk easier to swallow by reducing it as much as possible.

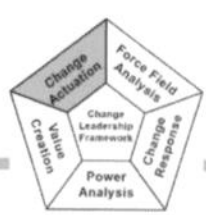


# SECRET # 84
# TWO ROOTS OF EVIL & FAILURE

*Communicate, communicate, and then communicate some more.*

*—Bob Nelson*

## WHAT I NEED TO KNOW

In the manufacturing and engineering worlds when something goes wrong, people try to understand why, so it can be fixed. The goal is to start with the symptom of the failure and work backward to find the original, or root, cause of the problem. If you performed failure analysis on all the projects that went "bad," you would likely find two root causes in most cases: insecurity and lack of communication. These two human frailties can sink any initiative.

In *Forceful Selling*, I discussed the notion that people are either fundamentally secure (S) or insecure (I)—what I called "Theory S" and "Theory I." Theory I people are dangerous because they easily feel threatened—and then they protect themselves by going on the attack. In the best case, their sometimes subtle and clandestine attacks put a huge drag on the change initiative. In the worst case, they succeed in dismantling it altogether.

The other common cause of failure is a failure to communicate. Theory I people may withhold information as a covert tactic. But, more often, communication errors are unintentional. People may be busy and neglect to communicate. Or people may fall prey to the false consensus bias whereby they assume other people have the same information and understanding as they themselves have.

## What I Need to Do

Be superattentive and vigilant in identifying behavior that is driven by insecurities or bad communication.

Identify insecurity-driven behavior by looking for common clues such as close-mindedness, aggressiveness, personal attacks, illogical reasoning, and unwillingness to listen.

Try to nip anxieties before they can bud: proactively reassure stakeholders of their position, their value, their importance to the success of the change, and how they will benefit from the change. Be specific and concrete in your statements. Fluffy, hand-waving assurances without specific facts will only inflame anxieties.

Err on overcommunicating views and status among stakeholders to avoid miscommunications.

Implement practices that stimulate stakeholders to share views frequently (e.g., weekly meetings, daily five-minute briefings, real-simple-syndication feeds, etc.).

## Action Summary

- Develop plans to mitigate anxieties.
- Develop plans to contain Theory I influence and damage.
- Implement practices to facilitate strong communication.

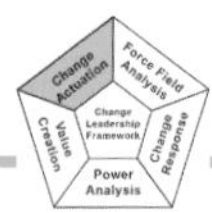


# SECRET # 85
# PERSEVERANCE WINS

*Great works are performed not by strength but by perseverance.*

*—Samuel Johnson*

## WHAT I NEED TO KNOW

All the biggest achievements of mankind have required perseverance that extended over decades. The Panama Canal, which lifts large freight-carrying boats over forty-eight miles of land between the Pacific and Atlantic Oceans, took thirty-four years to build. The Golden Gate Bridge in San Francisco is another great achievement. Joseph Strauss, the chief engineer who managed the building of the bridge, lobbied for more than ten years just to get political support to build it. Then, he worked another ten years building the structural support for the bridge.

Those are two of the biggest projects on earth. Your projects likely will not require decades of perseverance. However, projects always seem to take far longer than originally estimated and seem always to take a back seat to other priorities.

To succeed as a change agent, you must steadfastly pursue the change despite difficulties, obstacles, or discouragement. After all, if it were easy, someone else would have already done it, right?

The dilemma is knowing when you should persevere, and when you should cut your losses and disqualify the opportunity. The best way to handle this dilemma is not to ask "if" the customer will change, but "when."

## What I Need to Do

When the customer changes, you want to be the salesperson who is present to receive the order. Consider yourself a gardener tending to a tomato patch, rather than a hunter searching for ready-to-eat food. Not all tomatoes ripen at the same time. So the gardener nurtures them through their various stages of maturity until each is ready to harvest.

Just as it would be mind-numbing to sit and watch a single tomato grow, you will go crazy, and become poor, waiting for a specific customer to change. So, fill your garden with as many opportunities as you can nurture at once.

Don't stop looking for newer, better opportunities. As you identify better opportunities, you can prune the opportunities that seem to be rotting on the vine.

Keep in mind that your success ultimately depends on your ability to overcome difficulties and obstacles. A change agent with tremendous perseverance will be tremendously valuable to her customers.

## Action Summary

- Remain steadfast in your pursuit of creating value for the client.
- Nurture multiple opportunities.
- Always be looking for new opportunities.

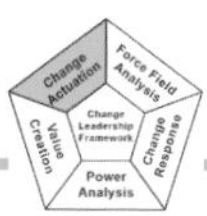


# Secret # 86
# Always Have Options

*On the human chessboard, all moves are possible.*
—*Miriam Schiff*

## What I Need to Know

If you are committed solely to one course of action, you will eventually perish. Even the smallest pebble will trip you up. For example, modern automobiles have rubber tires and shock absorbers that adapt to the road, enabling them to move at very high speeds. Without that capability, the smallest pebbles would reduce cars to a snail's pace.

In *The Art of War*, Sun Tzu talks about "The Nine Situations" of battle. He calls the situation where you have no options, "hemmed-in territory." He says you are very vulnerable in this situation and, therefore, you should avoid engaging the enemy. Of course, being in a vulnerable position without the ability to engage does not help you broker high-value deals or grow your business. If the enemy engages you on hemmed-in territory, Sun Tzu calls that situation "desperate ground." He says you are now in a struggle for your life. How can you avoid these situations and have many options?

Kurt Lewin says that people with bigger life spaces have more options available to them. Remember Lewin's example that a child may have difficulty feeding himself while an adult can explore the realms of gourmet cooking? You want to maximize your life space and to help the customer maximize his. You can move from the abstract notion of life space to concrete choices by using the Four Forces model as a guide.

## WHAT I NEED TO DO

Be flexible and adaptive. When conditions change, or when people have conflicting views, adapt to the situation. You are the change leader—it is not your role to be stuck to one option.

Try to play the role of the shock absorber in the automobile by inserting yourself between conflicting views—in other words, be a "broker" and a diplomat. A broker can often soften a message and depersonalize it, thereby helping the recipient acknowledge the validity of other options.

Explore and expand the customer's life space by utilizing the Four Forces model to identify more options.

Finally, Sun Tzu says that a battle cannot be won without information, strategy, and planning. Keep in mind that the change leader becomes a strategic resource when she provides outstanding counsel in these critical elements.

## ACTION SUMMARY

- Remain "open" to all ideas and options.
- Help keep the customer open to more options by brokering them.
- Use the Four Forces model to identify additional options.

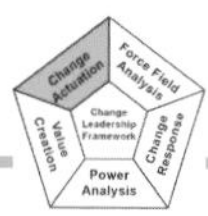


# SECRET # 87
# DEVELOP YOUR CHANGE TEAM

*It is amazing what you can accomplish if you do not care who gets the credit.*

*—Harry S. Truman*

## WHAT I NEED TO KNOW

In traditional solution-oriented selling, there is the concept of a sponsor. The sponsor is someone who believes your solution is the best and proactively helps you sell your solution to the company. The sponsor is essentially an internal salesperson for you. Having a sponsor is critically important for winning the business. You cannot win without one. The same is true for change leadership. You need one or more people who believe you can help the organization and are willing to help you succeed.

Traditional sales methods also talk about "calling high," "selling to power," identifying supporters versus enemies and the roles of various people on the buying committee (e.g., evaluator, recommender, decision maker, and approver). Calling high early in the sales cycle may work in simpler solution-oriented sales.

However, change-centric selling can involve much higher value and more complex initiatives that cross organizational boundaries. So change leadership involves a new vocabulary of terms such as stakeholders (instead of buying committee), internal change agent (instead of sponsor), and resource owners (instead of decision makers) to name a few examples.

Ultimately, you need to assemble a "change team" comprised of people who not only are now experiencing the forces of change, but who will later actuate the changes.

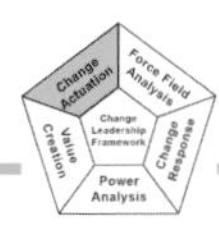




## WHAT I NEED TO DO

Recruit the following roles to your change team:

**Business owner**. The person responsible for achieving the revenue, cost, and mission goals of the organization. This person has the most strategic mindset and can set the vision for change.

**Internal change agent**. The person who wants to see you succeed and will obtain the authorization of the business owner to drive a change in the business.

**Resource owners**. The person(s) who controls resources either affected by the change or required to make the change. The success of the change project depends on the cooperation and execution of these resources.

**Resistance leader**. The person who is the voice of the resisting forces.

**Stakeholder leaders**. The person(s) who represents the various stakeholder groups who will be affected by the proposed change.

## ACTION SUMMARY

- Recruit people into each role of the change team.
- Identify the internal change agent as soon as possible.
- Build support for the change coalition through multiple iterations of individual contact.

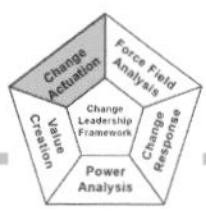


# SECRET # 88
# THERE'S NO FREE LUNCH

*Those who plow the sea do not carry the winds in their hands.*

*—Publilius Syrus*

## WHAT I NEED TO KNOW

Nobel Prize–winning economist Milton Friedman is associated with the famous phrase, "There is no such thing as a free lunch." Even if the lunch is advertised as free, someone is going to pay at some point—and ultimately, it is going to be you. This is also true of change. Whether a change is made, now, later, or never—there will be a price to pay. Inaction and missed opportunities are large costs, although they are often hidden or ignored—temporarily. The cost of making a change too quickly can be high. And the cost of making a change too slowly can be even higher. The first step in change actuation is acknowledging that these costs cannot be avoided. The next step is to determine what is achievable and appropriate.

**Scope, Schedule, and Resources**

Determining what changes are achievable is a matter of assessing the three constraints of project management.

**Scope**. Scope is essentially the "size" of the project.

**Schedule**. Schedule is the amount of time allotted to complete the project.

**Resources**. Resources required to complete a project include items such as labor, materials, capital equipment, expertise, processes, tools, and technology.

## WHAT I NEED TO DO

Help your client avoid these common "Where's the free lunch?" mistakes:

- Ignoring hidden costs
- Delaying action, hoping things will improve by themselves
- Underestimating the size of the project
- Underinvesting resources—expecting a project to be completed with few resources

Once the client has accepted the principle of "no free lunch," the change leader must help the client decide what configuration of scope, schedule, and resources constitutes an appropriate response to the forces of change. An "appropriate" change plan is the minimum scope, schedule, and resource configuration that implements the change.

Do not intentionally lowball the resource requirements and then later ask for more resources. You will lose the client's trust and the client will not rely on you as a strategic resource.

## ACTION SUMMARY

- Do not try to "plow the sea" and take on too much change.
- Drive objective analysis.
- Eliminate the "free lunch" assumptions and "magic happens here" steps in the change plan.

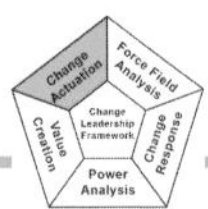


# Secret # 89
# Plan Ahead, But Deliver Version 1.0

*Everything should be made as simple as possible, but not simpler.*

*—Albert Einstein*

## What I Need to Know

People seem always to have "champagne tastes and beer budgets." They always want more than they are prepared to pay for. That's why we need to have "Version 1.0" in change leadership. "Version 1.0" is the set of the most important features and scope that are achievable as a first phase of the change. The other changes will have to wait until the next phase of the change process—they'll have to be "Version 2.0" changes.

One of the most common and fatal mistakes made by enthusiastic clients and change leaders is taking their attention off Version 1.0.

Once people buy into the vision of change, they want it all—not just what is in the first phase. So managers focus their attention on Version 2.0. This is a fatal mistake. Version 2.0 never comes. It never comes because the managers do not allow Version 1.0 to be completed. It's like a baseball batter focusing on the next pitch—the ball that hasn't been thrown yet—instead of the ball that is coming at him right now. Version 2.0 is nothing more than a dream, or a fantasy, until Version 1.0 becomes a reality.

A great change leader must emulate the intense concentration of great athletes like Tiger Woods, Lance Armstrong, and Cortez Kennedy. They get Version 2.0 accomplished, all right. In fact, they deliver Version 10.0—eventually. But the way they get there is by putting their full attention on the task at hand.

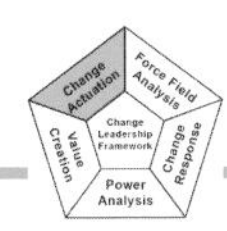




## WHAT I NEED TO DO

The only way to deal with scarce resources is to reduce the scope of the change. You can do this by breaking large change initiatives into multiple, achievable phases that deliver acceptable results along the way.

Then, as you are actuating the change, maintain the promise of Version 2.0 and future phases, but focus 100 percent of the client's energy on Version 1.0.

To maintain this focus is easier said than done because the client will put a lot of pressure on the change leader to deliver Version 2.0. This is another opportunity for you to demonstrate the discipline of high quality and high value—by remaining committed to the realities of the scope, schedule, and resource constraints and to the successful completion of Version 1.0—before entertaining discussions of Version 2.0.

## ACTION SUMMARY

- Break large initiatives into multiple, achievable phases.
- Plan all phases, but focus 100 percent of attention on the present phase.
- Maintain the vision and promise of future phases, but make sure each phase delivers value of its own.

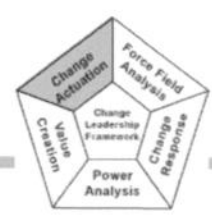


# Secret # 90
# Version 1.0 Is Junk

*Aim for success, not perfection. Never give up your right to be wrong, because then you will lose your ability to learn new things and move forward with your life.*

*—David M. Burns*

## What I Need to Know

Let's face it. Version 1.0 is a disappointment. Everyone bought into the vision of the change. At first, they were skeptical. But then they gradually saw the benefits and the driving forces and they eventually warmed up to the vision. Once the decision was made to move forward with the change and to define the implementation plan, people got downright enthusiastic. Then, when the implementation team came back with the plan for Version 1.0, it was like a dark storm cloud pouring rain all over the change parade. The implementation plan requires huge amounts of time and resources. In addition, key features of the change plan have been dropped due to costly obstacles.

That all sounds depressing, but the reality is that perfection is not possible. That does not mean you should resign yourself and your client to accepting low quality, or to giving up entirely. Rather, it means you have to accept the reality expressed in the verse from the Rolling Stones' song, "You can't always get what you want... You get what you need."

Your mindset as a change leader should be to strive for "Kaizen," the Japanese concept of continuous incremental improvement. In fact, incremental, rather than wholesale improvement is a core premise of quality control, because something cannot be controlled if more than one factor is changing at once.

## WHAT I NEED TO DO

Do not expect perfection on Day One, or on Version 1.0.

Rather than striving for the perfect, all-the-bells-and-whistles version, break up the change plan into smaller chunks that can be implemented in phases with measurable milestones.

Consider change as something that happens continuously and incrementally rather than suddenly and completely. Scale the increments according to the magnitude of the project scope and resources. For example, deploying software to 100,000 users would have bigger increments than deploying to 100 users.

Remember that quality control depends on the ability to measure the separate impact of each variable. Although enthusiastic customers may want to forge ahead all at once, if anything goes wrong (and you can bet something will), it may be much more difficult and costly to find the cause and correct it. A systematic, step-by-step approach usually gets the project completed faster and cheaper—even though it may seem more costly in the beginning.

## ACTION SUMMARY

- Do not aim for perfection—aim for incremental improvement.
- Identify appropriate milestones for the size of the change.
- Plan and execute the change in a systematic, step-by-step manner.

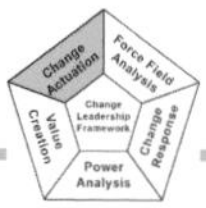


# SECRET # 91
# LEVERAGE CRITICS

*Any jackass can kick down a barn, but it takes a good carpenter to build one.*

*—Lyndon B. Johnson*

## WHAT I NEED TO KNOW

If there is a risk of enthusiastic clients over-estimating what is achievable, there is an even bigger risk that there will be a chorus of critics who say nothing is possible. Of course, you should address critics with a solid plan and concrete data. But they may attack your data and credibility, leading to a game of "he said—she said."

In *The Art of War,* Sun Tzu dedicates a full chapter to "The Use of Spies." He describes five kinds of spies:

1. **Local**. A person who has expertise in a certain area.
2. **Inward**. A person who works for the enemy, in this case the critics.
3. **Converted**. A spy originally in the employ of the enemy, but now in your employ.
4. **Doomed**. A person who is spying on you to whom you give erroneous information for that person to report to the enemy.
5. **Surviving**. A person who brings back information from the enemy.

It may be insightful to consider Sun Tzu's definitions and ponder who in your customer's organization may fit them.

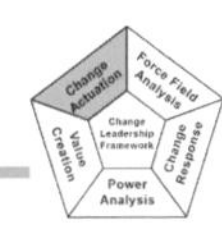




## What I Need to Do

Sun Tzu offers the following guidance for dealing with spies (I have substituted the word "critic" for "spy.").

There is no one in the organization with whom the leader should have a more intimate relationship than the critics. Also, no one in the organization should be more liberally rewarded by the leader.

Critics must be managed in straightforward and benevolent ways. Playing games with them will not engender the service you want.

Be careful in trusting information reported by the critics.

Use critics for every kind of business. But be very, very subtle in using information provided by critics. In no other business should greater secrecy be preserved.

You need to understand critics' views and how those views are circulated. Then, and only then, will you have all the information you need to formulate and communicate what changes are achievable. So, in keeping with your position of detachment and diplomacy, visit the critics often. Understand them. Convert them.

## Action Summary

- Identify people who are playing in the various spy roles.
- Embrace critics and understand them.
- Try to convert critics, or broker agreement with them.

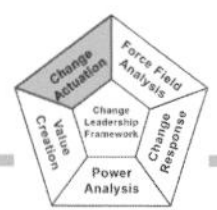


# Secret # 92
# Where There Is Change, There Is Conflict

*A diamond is a chunk of coal that made good under pressure.*

*—Anonymous*

## What I Need to Know

Business is war. Or at least, there are those who think it is. As a change agent, you are often at the front line of that war.

The bigger the perceived importance of the change you are involved with, the more crossfire to which you may be exposed. There are many ways and reasons that you can be hit by the crossfire. For example, people may think that if they can slow you down, they can slow down the change. Or they may see you as an agent of the "enemy."

Also, change can be an emotionally charged process, invoking powerful feelings associated with death and deeply seated anxieties. You may get caught in the middle of those internal conflicts and may even be a lightning rod for people's emotions.

Weathering those conflicts can be extremely difficult and taxing for the change agent. Symptoms of change agent fatigue include feelings of:

- **Isolation**—no one seems to be on your side
- **Helplessness**—nothing you do seems to work
- **Confusion**—not knowing what to do next
- **Questioning your value**—wondering whether you are wrong
- **Despair**—considering giving up

## What I Need to Do

First, don't take anything personally. This is easier said than done, unless you have a neurotic level of self-confidence. The best way to keep a cool head is to focus on staying aligned with your client.

Second, remain detached. This is not only a coping strategy to help in not taking the conflict personally; it is also a way to stay out of the conflict. If at times you feel as if you are in a professional football game on the line of scrimmage with 300-pound players all around you, imagine instead that you are in a press box high above the football stadium. Then, observe. Where are the players throwing their blocks? What play are they using from the playbook?

Third, fear not. As Franklin D. Roosevelt said, "The only thing we have to fear, is fear itself." This could not be truer than in change leadership. If you imagine yourself as a ghost or commentator high above the playing field, then you cannot get hurt and you will have nothing to fear. Being fearless and being unintimidated makes you a far more effective change agent.

## Action Summary

- Be prepared for conflict—don an imaginary bulletproof shield.
- Remain detached and do not participate in the conflict.
- Stay aligned with your client—she's the boss.

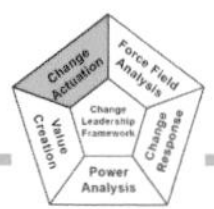


# Secret # 93
# Maintain Positive Momentum

*A word once let out of the cage*
*cannot be whistled back again.*
*—Horace (1st century B.C.)*

## What I Need to Know

One of the most powerful "forces" acting on a change initiative is the force of momentum. Momentum is technically not a force. But it can feel like a force with a life of its own.

Momentum is actually mass times velocity: $P = m v$

Think about pushing a stalled automobile. It takes a lot of force to get the car moving. But once it is moving, look out. It seems like it has a life of its own. The reason it seems alive is that the moving mass has its own energy (given by the equation, $E = ½mv^2$). So it's going to keep on moving until something pushes with equal energy to stop it. What does it feel like to get in front of the car and stop it? Difficult—to say the least.

In your role as change agent, you must actuate the change—you have to get the car moving. At first, the change seems impossibly heavy to move. But once it starts moving, every push makes it go faster, until it seems to take on a life of its own. The task then becomes steering and controlling it. These are the processes of change actuation.

The one situation you want to avoid is the momentum going against you. It literally takes twice the energy to turn around the momentum. Not only is it just as hard to push the car forward, but first, you have to stop it from running you over.

To actuate change successfully, you must establish positive momentum, no matter how small, from the very beginning.

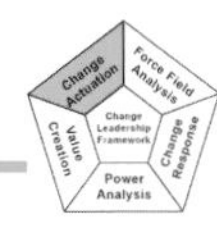




## WHAT I NEED TO DO

To make sure you establish positive momentum from the very beginning, wait to start actuating the change until you have lined up the support to power the change and overcome resistance.

During the coalition-building phase, consider keeping a low profile by "floating" "ideas" by stakeholders to determine their willingness to support various change options.

Determine the positive momentum (mass times velocity) that various stakeholders will contribute to the change coalition. The analogy of mass is their influence in the organization. The analogy of velocity is how quickly and forcefully they will support the change.

Calculate the negative momentum the resistors will invest in resisting the change.

Raise your profile and the awareness of the change proposal only after the positive momentum safely exceeds the negative.

## ACTION SUMMARY

- Maintain a healthy fear and respect of the influence of momentum.
- Carefully build momentum one stakeholder at a time.
- Actuate only after positive momentum is assured.

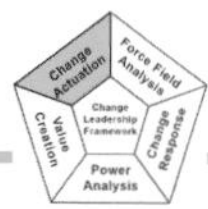


# SECRET # 94
# BE THE SKEPTIC WHO ALWAYS BELIEVES

*The clearest sign of wisdom is continued cheerfulness.*
*—Michel Eyquem de Montaigne*

## WHAT I NEED TO KNOW

In assessing and convincing stakeholders what is achievable, the change agent needs almost to have two personalities. One personality should be the promoter who inspires everyone to action with exciting visions of what is possible. The other personality should be the skeptic who questions what is realistic and achievable and sets expectations based on the philosophy of "underpromise and overdeliver."

Basically, one personality, or "role," needs to convince people to "buy" and the other personality needs to deliver. One reason a change leader is so much more valuable than a solution provider is that the change leader fulfills both roles. The change leader is operating objectively with the client's best interest in mind.

After all the healthy skepticism, objectivity, and enthusiasm, when it comes to change actuation, the change agent is "the device that develops force and motion from an available energy source." What is that energy source? It is that smiling fountain of energy that looks at you in the mirror. So above all, in order to actuate others, the change leader must fully believe in the changes she is leading. Think of yourself as Tom Sawyer in *The Adventures of Tom Sawyer* by Mark Twain. When Tom is asked to paint the long fence in front of the house, he does this laborious chore with such enthusiasm that he charges his friends for the privilege of painting the fence for him.

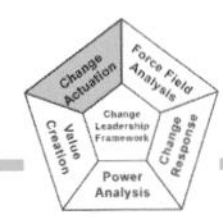



## What I Need to Do

Change-centric selling is very different from traditional selling where salespeople may be inclined to "dump and dash"—dumping the solution and dashing for the door.

Change-centric selling focuses on the change—the outcome—the customer is trying to achieve. Therefore, you cannot simply sell the customer an armful of goods and say, "Good luck with that." Your job is not done until the customer has successfully made the change.

Think of yourself as having two personalities. One personality is the skeptic who knows he must deliver on his commitments. The other personality is the actuator who energizes the customer and spurs him into action.

The trick is to balance these two perspectives and not fall into a rut where you overemphasize one over the other.

Remember: You must believe. And you must deliver.

## Action Summary

- Set realistic expectations and then exceed them.
- Identify motivated stakeholders who will actuate the change.
- Assume that you are the only source of energy you can count on.

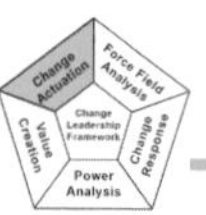


# SECRET # 95
# DRIVE CHANGE AWARENESS

*The first step toward change is awareness.*
*—Nathaniel Branden*

## WHAT I NEED TO KNOW

Change actuation begins with awareness. In *Forceful Selling,* I described five stages of change awareness:

1. **Unrecognized**. Either the person or organization has not recognized the need for a change, or is unaware of the proposed change.
2. **Recognized, but not prioritized**. Even once the need for a change has been recognized and a specific change has been proposed, it must still compete with the other needs and proposed changes that have been recognized by the person or organization.
3. **Prioritized**. If the proposed change has more driving forces and fewer resisting forces than other proposed changes, then it will be prioritized. Here, we define "prioritized" as having been assigned sufficient priority that the change plan is authorized and funded.
4. **In process**. The change plan has been actuated, but is not yet completed.
5. **Satisfied**. The change has been completed and the forces that drove the change have been satisfied.

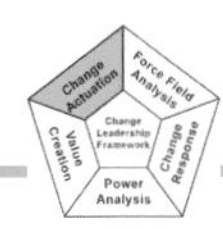




## What I Need to Do

You likely have limited influence on the priority of a specific change. If decision making in the organization is "efficient," then high-power changes will be prioritized over low-power changes.

So, spend your energy aligning with high-power changes rather than trying to convince stakeholders that a low-power change is really a high-power change. Do this by performing a thorough and accurate force field analysis and identifying the largest forces. Then, align with the changes those forces are driving.

Once you are aligned with the most powerful forces and changes, help your customer drive awareness of them by assembling a change team comprising key stakeholders.

After all the key stakeholders recognize the need for change, work with your change team to develop a change plan that can be driven through the organization's prioritization process. To ensure successful prioritization, make people "familiar" with the change plan by executing a broad awareness campaign that includes demonstrations and/or visualizations of the final outcome.

## Action Summary

- Align with high-power forces and changes.
- Help the customer drive initial awareness among key stakeholders.
- After a change plan is formulated, drive broad awareness of the final desired outcome.

# Secret # 96
# Recognize the Status Quo

*Choose always the way that seems best, however rough it may be; custom will soon render it easy and agreeable.*
*—Pythagoras*

## What I Need to Know

According to the Tannenbaum & Hanna model, the change process begins with the current state—the way things are now—the status quo. Three steps or categories of actions keep the current situation frozen.

**Homeostasis and Inertia**

Homeostasis is the ability and the processes that organisms use to maintain a stable condition. Inertia is the notion that people will eventually become comfortable with a situation, regardless of its desirability. Homeostatic processes and inertia not only maintain stability, they also tend to freeze the person's life space and inhibit change.

**Holding On**

In the frozen state, people are still holding on to the current situation. They do not want a change—they want to keep things just the way they are. This is a natural outcome of homeostasis. If people change too often, we see them as neurotic.

**Defense Mechanisms**

At this stage, people reinforce their "holding on" by erecting defenses around the status quo. They appraise the current state using deny, devalue, and delay coping strategies. And they may emote with destructive and distracting emotions.

## WHAT I NEED TO DO

Your key task at this stage is to identify and characterize the status quo.

It is important to note that in some cases, the change process will stop right here. In other words, it will stop before it ever has a chance to get started. How many people do you know who have built castle walls around themselves as impregnable as the City of Troy? They are the Turtles who withdraw into their shells and refuse even to talk about the subject of a proposed change. Lewin notes that these people must experience a catharsis before they can unfreeze their life space.

Rather than exhaust your resources trying to convince a Turtle to change, or waiting for a cathartic event that may never come, you will be more successful if you disqualify the Turtles from your pipeline. If one of the stakeholders in an organization is a Turtle, you will need to review your power analysis and make an "over-through-around" decision regarding the Turtle.

## ACTION SUMMARY

- Develop a thorough understanding of the status quo.
- Identify what will be changing.
- Understand the mechanisms and forces with which people are holding on and defending the status quo.

# Secret # 97
# Unfreeze the Status Quo

*The time is always right to do what is right.*
*—Martin Luther King, Jr.*

## What I Need to Know

The second stage of the change process is to unfreeze the current state.

### Dying

The person must let his dream and desire to keep forever the status quo die. Elisabeth Kübler-Ross developed the famous Five Stages of Grief model:

1. **Denial**. "This cannot be happening to me."
2. **Anger**. "Why did this happen to me? It's not fair!"
3. **Bargaining**. "Let's make a deal and say this never happened."
4. **Depression**. "I have nothing. I don't know what to do."
5. **Acceptance**. "I don't like it. But it really happened."

### Letting Go

Once people have accepted the impending end of the status quo, they must ultimately let go of it. Letting go is the last act of unfreezing the current situation. It is the stage when the chains have been cut, the knots have been untied, and the bonds have been melted. At this point, the resistors have given up their efforts to keep the change proposal from being accepted. They must now get out of the way or get squashed. Of course, they may still throw sand in the gears and try other ways to sabotage the change, but at this point, they cannot stop it from starting.

## WHAT I NEED TO DO

As a change leader, you should be aware that these stages are important processes that the client must, in many cases, traverse before the actual change process can be initiated.

It is often difficult for people to pull themselves from one stage to the next without external help. Your role will be to gently usher your client through each stage, enabling him to release the emotions, but also ensuring he does not get stuck in a stage.

These stages are all loaded with emotion, so steel yourself for a potentially bumpy ride with the client.

People recovering from addiction or the death of a loved one are not the only people who go through these stages; you do not have to be an addiction or hospice counselor to find yourself in the middle of an emotionally charged situation. Many people invest the majority of their self-esteem in their jobs and, therefore, perceive their very livelihoods are at stake. Take the stages as seriously as your client does.

Retain your sanity by retaining your own emotional detachment.

## ACTION SUMMARY

- Monitor the customer through the unfreezing process.
- Be prepared for high emotions.
- Provide support, as appropriate, to pull the customer from one stage to the next.

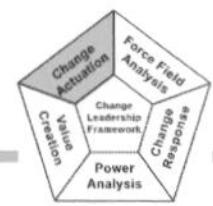


# Secret # 98
# Make the Change

*Many of life's failures are people who did not realize how close they were to success when they gave up.*

*—Thomas Edison*

## What I Need to Know

The third stage of change actuation is actually making the change. This stage is accompanied by the following processes.

**Confusion**

Once action begins, people ask all the questions. Who's on first? Who's on second? What did we say we were going to do about this? How are we doing that?

**Rebirth**

This is the step of creating the new state. The new house must be built before the family can be moved out of the old house. As the new house is built, as the change takes shape, the new state comes to life. The emptiness associated with the end of the status quo is replaced by a new situation that is, well, actually refreshing.

**Moving On**

The game was finally afoot—now, it is finally over. People have settled into the new house. Just as there was an acceptance of the end of the current situation, there is now acceptance of the new situation.

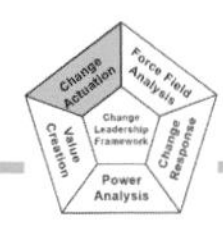


## What I Need to Do

The change leader needs to be cautious regarding a potential pothole that could trip up the change process. Lewin cites research that shows people tend to slow down as they reach a goal. Before the change process starts, the person is stationary. Then the person decides to make the change and steps into the starting blocks like a sprinter. Something triggers actuation and the person gets off to a good start. But as the finish line gets closer, the person slows down. Apparently, the farther away people are from a goal, the harder they feel they have to work. The closer they are, the less they feel they have to work.

Lewin and Maslow both talk about how once a person achieves a goal, the person is not satisfied. The goal the person had longed for so much creates an empty feeling once it is achieved. The person immediately feels unsatisfied and sets another goal.

Make sure the client completely achieves the present goal before he moves on!

## Action Summary

- Be extremely well-organized and systematic during this stage.
- Err on overcommunicating status and progress.
- Don't let up your effort until the last detail has been completed.

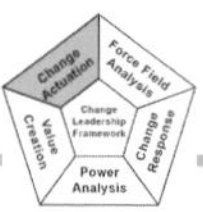

# SECRET # 99
# POUR THE CONCRETE

*Nothing will work unless you do.*

*—Maya Angelou*

## WHAT I NEED TO KNOW

After the change is completed, the new situation starts to become the status quo. Roots start to sprout and people start to become entrenched, again.

But often there are forces pulling the change back to the former status quo. Some changes require constant reinforcement. Some changes feel like you are perpetually pushing that ore cart full of gold uphill. As soon as you think it is stable, it slowly starts to move backward. There are many reasons the change could tend back to the original state.

Even if the client is very happy with the change, he is still subject to the human tendency to feel some question or regret. This tendency, called "buyer's remorse," is when a person comes home with his shiny new widget he has wanted for so long and regrets that he purchased it. Many big consumer brands collectively spend billions of dollars on advertising, with the express purpose of—not convincing customers to buy the product—but rather, convincing them after they bought it that they did the right thing.

There's a similar phenomenon called the "winner's curse." This is the dilemma that the buyer must have paid too high of a price, because the seller accepted it. There is also the dilemma that the seller must have accepted too low of a price because the buyer was willing to pay. The only way to be sure the price is not too high or too low is if the other side walks away from the bargaining table. So even the happiest client needs encouragement and affirmation.

## What I Need to Do

Another cause of buyer's remorse and potential regression to the status quo could be resistors and critics. No change goes perfectly, and you can always count on the critics to say, "See! See! I told you it wouldn't work!" This is the time to remind everyone of the benefits of the change and all of the progress that has been made.

In some cases, by the time the change has been completed, other changes have occurred that reduce the effectiveness and benefits of the change. In these cases, the client either must accept the change as it is or modify it. Either option the client chooses will require additional effort—reinforcement to keep the change from going backward.

At some point, after the change has been long since accepted and the reinforcements have locked it in place, people adapt and become comfortable, building castle walls around the new status quo. The change cycle then starts anew. As Maslow says, "Man is a perpetually wanting animal." The satisfaction of one need creates a dissatisfaction with another. Prepare to satisfy the next "need."

## Action Summary

- Reinforce the benefits and achievements.
- Adapt to changing conditions by making additional modifications.
- Quickly move forward to the next change, as the person becomes aware of the next need.

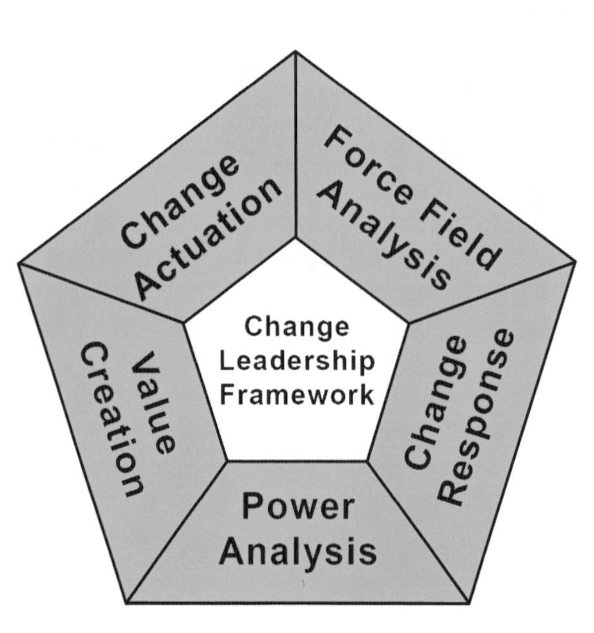
Change Actuation
Force Field Analysis
Change Leadership Framework
Value Creation
Change Response
Power Analysis

# CHANGE AGENT

## BEING A CHANGE AGENT

# INTRODUCTION

# TO

# BEING A CHANGE AGENT

Now that we have covered the five disciplines of the Change Leadership Framework, this section discusses some tips, tricks, and land mines that apply across all of the disciplines of change leadership.

### What is it?

A change agent is someone who operates as a counselor, consultant and leader to help the client achieve his or her goals.

Change leadership is counterintuitive in that the change leader must lead where the followers want to go. That is why the concept of a change "agent" is more appropriate; that is, a person employed by the customer to achieve the customer's desired outcomes.

### Why is it important?

You will succeed only if you lead where the customer wants to go.

People will only do something if they feel motivation. That is the reason developing a deep understanding of the forces that motivate your customers is so critical for spurring them to action.

### How is it new or different?

Good salespeople operate as consultants, helping the customer find the best solution to satisfy his need. Great salespeople operate as agents who proactively seek opportunities to help the customer succeed. In a legal context an agent is someone who is authorized to take action for a person's benefit. If you live by this philosophy and consistently deliver high value, your customers will begin to rely on you as their trusted advisor.

## What are the common misconceptions?

There is a common perception that a change agent is someone who shakes up an organization and forcefully drives people where they don't want to go. If you want to lead people where they don't want to go, you should study books on hypnosis, mind control and other coercion techniques. Those techniques rarely lead to high customer satisfaction and deep, highly profitable, long-term relationships

You will be far more successful by operating as a counselor to help your customers identify their feelings, understand how they are responding, and make the choices that create the most benefit for them.

## What are the key take-aways & how do I put them in action?

Think of yourself not as a need-satisfaction consultant, but rather as an agent employed by the customer to lead change and create value. Start by understanding what the customer values and where the customer wants to go.

By becoming an adept agent of change, you will deliver irresistible value to your customers that your competitors won't even understand. You will then become a resource that your customers will come to rely on and value highly.

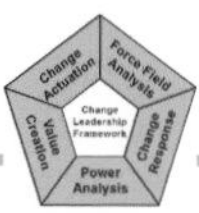


# Secret # 100
# Building Value Takes Time

*He that can have patience can have what he will.*
*—Benjamin Franklin*

## What I Need to Know

Would you like customers to go ahead and place the order today, rather than next week, next quarter, or next year? Do you wish you were a bulldog salesperson who could tug the order through the customer's approval process now, rather than at the customer's seemingly excruciatingly slow speed?

One of the biggest mistakes executives make is attempting to accelerate the buying cycle faster than the customer's natural pace will allow. The situation is similar to swimming against a current where despite your best efforts, you do not move very far ahead. On the other hand, if you swim with the current, at the customer's pace, you can get a much better result with fewer resources.

There is a more fundamental dilemma, though. As always, everything has a cost. The cost of building high value is that it requires more time. Conversely, the cost of going after quick business is that the margins will be lower and there will be more competitors. You didn't think you were the only person wanting a quick buck, did you?

So, you are faced with what might be called the "Salesperson's Dilemma": Should you take more, lower-margin, more competitive, faster-closing deals? Or should you take fewer, higher-margin, less competitive, slower-closing deals? Only you can answer that. But, two things are certain: (1) building more value takes more time than building less value, and (2) you are reading the wrong book if you want to quickly close low-margin deals—you should be learning about Internet marketing instead of change-centric selling.

## What I Need to Do

If you are a salesperson wondering why you care about high margins versus low margins, the answer is your commissions ultimately come from the margins. Companies that are not profitable after paying their salespeople eventually must find a lower cost sales channel or they will go out of business. Either way, you will be getting unemployment checks instead of commission checks. So if you want fat commissions, you have to generate fat margins.

The really great thing about pursuing the path of building high value is that you eventually reach a tipping point where you (a) have developed a track record of high-value delivery and (b) your resources are fully utilized on high-value deals. From that point forward you become resource constrained, rather than order constrained. You will literally be booking business faster than you can deliver it, which enables you to cherry pick the highest margin opportunities. Your profits will start soaring!

Of course, that all takes time. Just take it one step at a time...and you'll get there.

## Action Summary

- Follow the natural pace of the customer to get the biggest order.
- Increase your value delivery over time.
- Be careful not to tie up resources with low-margin business.

# Secret # 101
# Don't Skip Steps

*It is easier to do a job right than to explain why you didn't.*
*—Martin Van Buren*

## What I Need to Know

Wouldn't it be nice if you could just skip to the end? It would be nice, when you are in a boring departmental meeting, if you could just press the fast-forward button as people spoke and then hit the play button just as the department head says, "Okay, that's it for today. Thanks everybody."

Wouldn't it be nice if you could just "call high" and go right to the decision maker to get the purchase order and then move on to the next sale?

Bulldog salespeople might be able to skip steps and go for the quick close in transactional selling situations. But if you are establishing high value as a salesperson and high value for your product, you will not be successful in skipping steps.

Value perception is like a chain where every link is the value perceived by a person on the buying committee. Your ability to pull the order through the customer's approval process depends on the strength of the chain. And the chain is only as strong as the person with the weakest perception of your value. The people who do not see the value will ultimately slow down your order. The worst-case scenario is that, in the process of questioning the value, they move themselves into a corner where they feel they must actively oppose your order just to preserve their credibility.

## WHAT I NEED TO DO

You will be far more successful if you cross every 't' and dot every 'i' in the process of establishing value. Moving fast in a competitive world is important, but no longer sufficient.

What matters most to buyers in today's competitive world?

Outcomes.

Features, benefits, solutions, and pricing can all be found in the four corners of the earth with the click of a computer mouse. The one, all-important item that cannot be delivered through a fiber-optic cable or by a parcel delivery truck is the actual outcome the customer is trying to achieve. Only the customer, with your assistance as her change agent, can achieve the outcome.

Determine the customer's desired outcome and then take every step necessary to achieve it—not one step more and not one step less.

## ACTION SUMMARY

- Make sure every link in the value chain supports your proposal.
- Focus on the customer's desired outcome.
- Determine the necessary steps and systematically complete them.

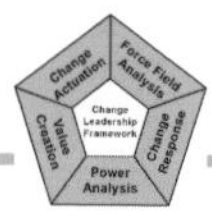


# Secret # 102
# People Must Learn on Their Own

*The real voyage of discovery consists not in seeking new landscapes, but in having new eyes.*

*—Marcel Proust*

## What I Need to Know

Do you wish your kids would listen to you? Why is it that when you say, "Don't touch the burner, or you'll get burned," they proceed to touch the burner? The frustration can be excruciating.

It would be nice if your children were just in a developmental stage and at some point they simply "grew out of it." But the reality is that they become adults—who still do not listen. Do you think you, the parent, are immune to this trait? Think about this: Do your parents listen to you? They are parents. But they can be as stubborn as teenagers or two-year-olds. Apparently, it is an inescapable human trait to have to learn by one's own mistakes, rather than by the mistakes of others.

In your role as a change agent, you may advocate until you are blue in the face. But the stakeholders may not be listening. They think they know better, that you are exaggerating, or that you do not fully understand. "That burner is not hot. How do you know it's hot? What do *you* know? My fingers feel fine. I'm not worried about a little burner...OW!! THAT HURTS!!" Only after they feel the sting for themselves will they believe you.

The important question for the change agent becomes, "How and when will the stakeholders feel the pain?" In other words, "What event will be the catalyst for action?"

## What I Need to Do

First, determine if stakeholders are really listening. Is the message going in one ear and out the other? Or have they fully internalized the forces at play?

Second, if you believe the customer fully appreciates the need for change, ask him what event caused his "a-ha" moment. If he cannot describe a past experience that enables him fully to appreciate the need, then his conviction will be limited.

If the customer appears not to be listening, immediately cease and desist with your advocacy and switch into inquiry mode. You need to inquire into the customer's views and identify an event that will be a catalyst for recognition and action.

Do not fool yourself by thinking your superior powers of persuasion and advocacy will convince the customer—as the CEO of a customer once told the VP of Sales at my company, "You're just a sales guy. What do you know?"

The only thing that matters is the pain in the customer's finger.

## Action Summary

- Focus on inquiry rather than advocacy.
- Identify the catalytic event.
- Preserve your resources until the event occurs.

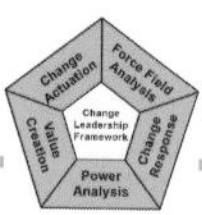


# Secret # 103
# Determine the Owner

*Leadership: the art of getting someone else to do something you want done because he wants to do it.*

*—Dwight D. Eisenhower*

## What I Need to Know

Who owns the problem? Who has the need? If you have a child, you have probably said, "You need to pick up your clothes and put them in the hamper before you go to bed." Did your child respond by saying, "Um...Actually, Dad, I don't really have a need for that. But, if you feel a need and it'll make you happy, sure I'll do a favor for you."

Has your child ever said in the morning, "Dad! I need my favorite shirt. Did you wash it? Where is it?" And then, you answered, "It's probably still where you left it in the corner of your room on the floor. I didn't have a need to look for it, so I didn't wash it."

It's often easy to forget who owns the problem and has the need. In the stereotypical example of asking children to clean up after themselves, most often, it is the parent who owns the need for cleanliness. The child does not feel the need. Conversely, parents often feel the need for washing clothes, when it is really the child who feels the need to have clean clothes. These misplaced needs are classic in organizations.

Countless times a day someone in one group will go to another group in an organization and say, "I need [something]." The other group's cooperation is less than enthusiastic because it does not feel any ownership or need. This happens although the organization's fundamental purpose is to divide labor, combine efforts, and achieve cooperatively what cannot be achieved individually.

## What I Need to Do

As you apply the disciplines of the Change Leadership Framework, identify and attach owners to each item. For example, as you analyze how the forces fan out through the organization, attach an owner to each force at each node. Then ask, "Why does this person feel he owns this?" This will give you a really good understanding of the organizational dynamics, which is instrumental in planning your coalition-building strategy.

Another example of sorting out ownership is assessing the Formula for Change in the power analysis discipline: Who owns the dissatisfaction? Who owns the vision for the new situation? Who will own the first steps?

These ownership questions are critical because action does not happen by itself. A specific person or group must ultimately take action. Who will take ownership and action?

Every aspect of the Change Leadership Framework involves ownership. Identify owners for each, being sure you accurately sort out the real ownership and avoid misplacing needs.

## Action Summary

- Be aware of misplaced needs.
- Identify the real owners for all aspects of the change.
- Remember, "He who takes ownership takes action."

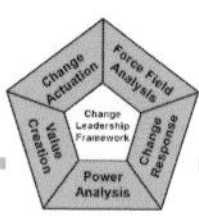


# Secret # 104
# Focus on the Method, Not the Effort

*Never mistake motion for action.*

*—Ernest Hemingway*

## What I Need to Know

We all have pressures that make us desperately want to grow our business. When looking for ways to grow our revenue, it is tempting to measure the activities of salespeople. But it's far more important to measure their strategies.

For example, I once was brought in to run a sales organization in a company that sold multimillion-dollar supercomputers for which there was a market of about ten very large companies with names such as Intel. One of the first things I did was ask my salespeople to show me their account plans. They said they did not have any account plans. The previous vice president of sales had told them, "It's a numbers game. I want you making five cold calls per day." Who else besides those ten large companies did he think was going to buy a supercomputer? Did he really believe the salespeople could dial random people in the phone directory and find someone who would answer the phone and say, "Sure, I could totally use a supercomputer for my business, right now. That would be like, totally radical, dude! Charge it to my Amex." It was a lot easier for that sales executive to measure sales activity than the quality and soundness of the sales strategy.

The reality is, it is always easier to measure activity than strategy. Developing and practicing sales methods and strategies are not easy endeavors. But, they have a far larger influence on success than sheer effort.

Effort *is* really important—*if* you have a winning strategy and a winning action plan.

## What I Need to Do

Rather than focusing on measuring effort, use these tactics to grow your sales:

- Hire motivated people and keep them motivated with appropriate incentives.
- Measure the effectiveness of strategies and the efficiency of tactics.
- Develop a robust set of qualification criteria and critical success factors for determining customers' readiness and willingness to purchase and use your offering.
- Allocate your resources to the customers who score the highest on qualification criteria and critical success factors.
- Build an organization to deliver high value and measure value-delivery activity, rather than prospecting activity.
- Commit yourself and your organization to the continuous study and improvement of these tactics.

## Action Summary

- Effort without strategy is like wind without a sail.
- Effort is easy. Strategy is hard. Focus on the strategy first, execution second.
- Focus on delivering value, rather than looking for it. But even then focus on the method, not the effort.

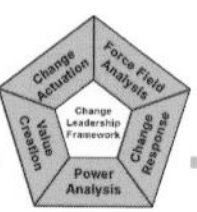


# SECRET # 105
# LEAVE TRANSACTIONAL SELLING FOR WEBSITES

*These days man knows the price of everything,*
*but the value of nothing.*

*—Oscar Wilde*

## WHAT I NEED TO KNOW

At the beginning of this book, I discussed how the forces of globalization and Internet commerce are reducing the perceived value of the traditional role of the sales professional, that is, to inform the customer and transact the purchase. What happens when a salesperson's perceived value diminishes—in other words, when the salesperson's value gets commoditized?

Salespeople are like the canaries in a mine. They are the early warning system for the health of your company and its competitiveness in the market. When the salesperson's value to the customer diminishes, so does the value of your product and your entire company. When your company's perceived value goes down, usually your revenues, margins, and profits follow.

Earlier, I posed the question of the Salesperson's Dilemma—whether to pursue easier low-margin business or more difficult high-margin business. At the top level of the company, the question does not have to be an either/or proposition. If your strategy requires that you do both, you just need to take two actions to be competitive:

1. Move transactional selling and low margin business to your website.
2. Upgrade the skills of your human sales force to a change-centric selling approach.

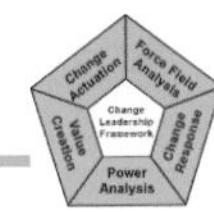



## WHAT I NEED TO DO

If your strategy is to move your sales to your website, you'll need to become an expert in online marketing.

If your strategy is to preserve the value of your sales force and you want to upgrade its ability to deliver high value, follow these steps:

- Survey the marketplace for sales methodologies designed specifically for selling high value.
- Look for a cogent framework that has a strong theoretical foundation, rather than shallow, 1-2-3 catchphrases.
- Make sure the methodology includes a strong set of tools, techniques, and job aids for implementing the framework in daily practice across the organization.
- Develop a "learning path" that defines a multiyear curriculum for salespeople to develop requisite skills over time.
- Implement the strategy in phases, monitoring and refining after each milestone.

## ACTION SUMMARY

- Move low-margin, transactional sales to your website.
- Develop a learning path and acquire the requisite skills.
- Take the first step today—the Internet does not sleep.

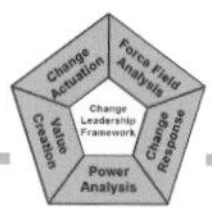

# SECRET # 106
# FOLLOW THE CHANGE LEADER CODE OF CONDUCT

*The simplest ethical precept is to be served by others as little as possible and to serve others as much as possible.*

*—Leo Tolstoy*

## WHAT I NEED TO KNOW

The change leader shall diligently:

1. Work as an agent authorized by the client to harness the forces of change on his or her behalf to achieve the client's desired result.
2. Do no harm.
3. Minimize the tension and cost of change.
4. Advise the client with objective and unbiased information, providing a balanced view of opportunity and risk.
5. Remain emotionally unattached.
6. Avoid becoming a stakeholder in the change.
7. Maintain leadership credibility.
    - Provide vision beyond the limits of the client's view.
    - Be trustworthy, operating in the client's best interest and making only positive changes.
    - Operate in a competent manner and ensure that competent expertise is brought in as appropriate.
8. Conduct him/herself according to the change leader behavior profile (see opposite page).

## What I Need to Do

### *Change Leader Profile*

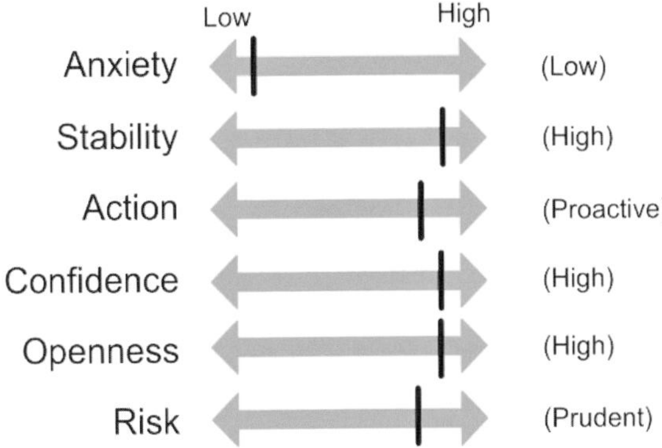


## Action Summary

- Work in the client's best interest.
- Be a credible leader.
- Behave as an ideal change leader.

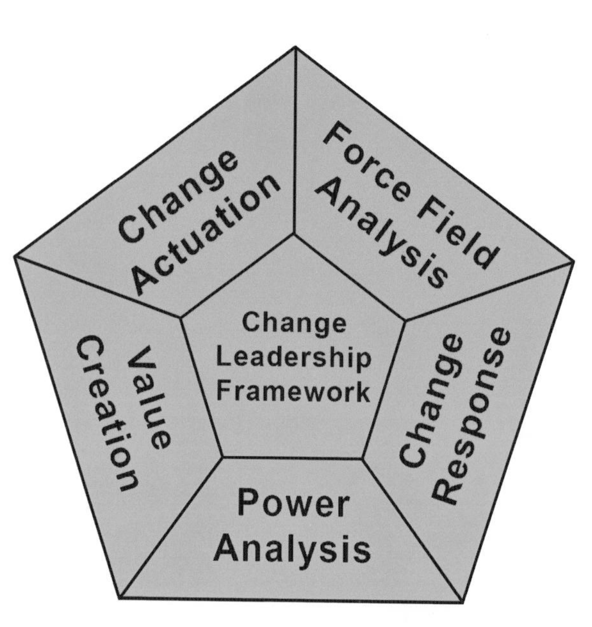
Change Actuation
Force Field Analysis
Change Leadership Framework
Value Creation
Change Response
Power Analysis

# CONCLUSION

## TAKING ACTION

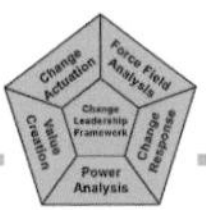


# SECRET # 107
# IT'S UP TO YOU

*Nobody can contribute to the best of humanity that does not make the best of himself.*

*—Johan Gottfried Herder*

## WHAT I NEED TO KNOW

Now that you have learned all the disciplines required to be an outstanding change leader, you need to take action.

I have given you a strong set of concepts and tools I have found to be extremely valuable based on my experience and research. Taken together, they form the most powerful sales methodology on the market today. Now it is time for you to implement this in your life. And when you do, you will rise to the top. You will achieve President's Club, Winner's Circle, qualify for the Hawaii trip, maximize your personal income and be the top earner—but only if you take action on this information and apply it to your accounts and prospective clients.

You can read the best diet and health books in the world. But you cannot lose weight by reading. You have to take action and apply the principles. Only by applying and living the principles in your business, your sales organization, your personal life, and with your customers will you be able to take control and harness the forces of change.

The more you exercise the principles in this book, the stronger your change leadership skills will become.

## What I Need to Do

Keep this book with you every day in your briefcase, on the plane, on your nightstand, and read a secret every day. Then, implement that secret at least once during the day.

Use the ribbon bookmark provided. Bend the pages. Use your yellow highlighter. Put marks on the concepts that strike a chord. Note the items you should be doing but are not. Prioritize the concepts and put numbers on the ones you will implement first. Now is the time to take action.

The ball is in your court. I challenge you to get started today—don't delay!

Be the Agent of Change!

## Action Summary

- Make change a part of everything you do.
- Become a student of change.
- Practice, practice, practice, and become the best change leader you can be.

# INDEX

*Page numbers followed by the letter "q" refer to quotations.*

## A



## B

## C

## M



## N



## O



## P

# NEXT STEPS

## FOR LEADING CHANGE

## &

## GROWING SALES

# ABOUT THE CHANGE LEADERSHIP GROUP®

Brett Clay is CEO of Change Leadership Group, LLC a management consulting and training firm focused on improving the business productivity of sales organizations and their clients.

## SALES ORGANIZATION DEVELOPMENT

Change Leadership Group offers a number of services to help clients develop the change leadership abilities of their sales organizations.

### *Training Courses*

In order to institutionalize the ChangeCentric Selling® methodology, CLG offers a comprehensive three-day boot camp followed by one year of Follow-Thru Consulting™. The first day covers the psychology of change in people and organizations. The second day covers value creation and negotiation. During the third day, each student learns to use the account planning tools and develop a real account plan for his most important account. CLG also offers an abbreviated two-day course and a one-day introductory course that could be appended to a conference.

### *Follow-Thru Consulting™*

In order for a sales method to become integrated into an organization's everyday behavior, three items are required. First, management must be committed to implementing the methodology. Second, the organization must use the tools and job aids as the primary means of collaboration and communications among the sales team members. Third, the methodology should be reviewed and reinforced periodically by the organization with special attention paid to best-practice sharing. Therefore, in order to ensure CLG clients' success, each training class includes follow-up visits and consulting for one year.

***Speaking and Seminars***
CLG instructors are also available for short, one-hour speaking engagements and three-hour seminars. For example, Brett Clay often speaks at industry conferences about delivering added value through change leadership.

## MANAGEMENT CONSULTING

Application of the Change Leadership Framework® for strategic planning and business performance optimization.

Change Leadership Group provides three offerings to help clients with strategic planning and business performance improvement.

***Strategic Planning***
CLG offers consulting services utilizing the Change Leadership Framework® to assess a company's situation, to determine the optimal strategy and to develop a plan for change. Because the framework assesses both the forces driving an organization and the processes for implementing change, it is a valuable tool for improving business performance.

***Facilitation Services***

Clients often request that CLG facilitate strategic planning meetings using the Change Leadership Framework®. The framework enables management teams to take a hard, fresh look at their business and leave the meeting with new insights and strong action plans.

***Executive Coaching***
Strategic plans must be mapped to specific action plans and strong follow-through to come to fruition. Utilizing CLG's Change Leadership Framework® for implementing change, CLG provides ongoing change leadership coaching and tuning of clients' change plans.

# Be published in Brett Clay's next book

## Share your secret of success with other readers!

- Do you have a habit that makes you highly effective?
- Have you learned a lesson that you live by?
- Do you see many people making the same mistake?
- What idea are you really passionate about?

**Submitting your secret to be published is easy!**

The format is the same as *Selling Change*. Just write *What I Need to Know* in 250 words and *What I Need to Do* in 200 words. Then, go to www.SellingChange.com to complete the submission form.

If your secret is approved, your name and biographical information will appear with the secret in the book!

**Join the ranks of other highly successful executives and salespeople who have already submitted their secrets.**

**Don't delay—the publishing deadline is coming fast.**

**www.SellingChange.com**

# 50% Discount on *Selling Change* flashcards

## with purchase of book.

**If you bought this book, simply go to www.SellingChange.com and enter the promotional code at checkout.**

**enter promo code: 1Y32H4**

Mem-Cards® are fast-reading, pocket-sized cards that you can use as a quick reminder or as a training tool for your sales or management team. Each deck contains the key ideas extracted from *Selling Change*, including summaries of 25 secrets.

Fun, fast, and easy to use, Mem-Cards are the answer to the information overload age we live in. Use them for yourself or buy them for friends and co-workers—they make the perfect gift!

**www.SellingChange.com**

## ABOUT THE AUTHOR

Brett Clay is CEO of Change Leadership Group, LLC, a management consulting and training firm focused on improving the business performance of sales organizations and their clients. He is an author, international speaker, sales trainer, consultant, and a veteran of twenty years in international sales and marketing management. He has held vice president roles in sales, business development, and marketing at numerous high-technology companies and was most recently at Microsoft Corp. His broad industry experience ranges from enterprise software to the computers that run the software to the silicon chips that make up the computers. He is the author of *Forceful Selling, How You Can Achieve Explosive Growth by Harnessing the Forces of Change,* which is a study in the psychology of change and the forces that drive it. Brett holds a Master of Business Administration degree from Santa Clara University and a Bachelor of Science degree in electrical engineering from Colorado State University and is a certified project management professional.